KARATE'S History and Traditions

REVISED EDITION

KARATE'S History and Traditions

REVISED EDITION

BRUCE A. HAINES

CHARLES E. TUTTLE COMPANY
Rutland, Vermont & Tokyo, Japan

空手拳法唐手功夫空
手拳法唐手功夫空手
拳法唐手功夫空手拳

空
手

拳法唐手功夫空手拳
法唐手功夫空手拳法
唐手功夫空手拳法唐
手功夫空手拳法唐手
功夫空手拳法唐手功
夫空手拳法唐手功夫
空手拳法唐手功夫空
手拳法唐手功夫空手
拳法唐手功夫空手拳
法唐手功夫空手拳法
唐手功夫空手拳法唐
手功夫空手拳法唐手
功夫空手拳法唐手功
夫空手拳法唐手功夫
空手拳法唐手功夫空
手拳法唐手功夫空手
拳法唐手功夫空手拳
法唐手功夫空手拳法
唐手功夫空手拳法唐
手功夫空手拳法唐手
功夫空手拳法唐手功
夫空手拳法唐手功夫
空手拳法唐手功夫空
手拳法唐手功夫空手
拳法唐手功夫空手拳
法唐手功夫空手拳法
唐手功夫空手拳法唐
手功夫空手拳法唐手
功夫空手拳法唐手功
夫空手拳法唐手功夫
空手拳法唐手功夫空

Published by the Charles E. Tuttle Company, Inc.
of Rutland, Vermont & Tokyo, Japan
with editorial offices at
2-6 Suido, l-chome, Bunkyo-ku, Tokyo

LCC Card No. 68-25893
ISBN 0-8048-1947-5

First edition, 1968
First revised paperback edition, 1995
Third printing, 1997

Printed in Singapore

To

Dr. Minoru Shinoda

Contents

ILLUSTRATIONS

PREFACE

MY INITIAL interest in karate and other Asian martial arts started in 1954. At that time, I became a student of William Chow at the Nuuanu YMCA in Honolulu. From that point to the present time, through three different karate schools, numerous instructors, twenty-five years of kendo training and competition, and a master's thesis on the history of karate taken at the University of Hawaii, my attitude towards all martial arts has evolved from naive interest and dedication to a position of frustration, hostility, general indifference, and again bewildering amazement. This is due to the various stages that karate and its similar "cousins" have gone through, and are continuing to evolve through. America's initial ignorance of karate per se, and its generally related arts, produced an aura surrounding karate that was both fictional and sensational.

From the 1950s to the 1990s, the takeoff of karate enthusiasm was astounding. In 1954, few Japanese knew of karate, and those that did considered it a foreign (Okinawan) import. Because the Allied Occupational authorities after World War II considered it to be some kind of Chinese exercise, it was not outlawed like the other purely Japanese fighting arts. Some claim it was allowed because American GIs wanted to learn karate to improve their own fighting skills. This enabled karate to start on its remarkable journey.

Today, hundreds of millions of people all over the globe not only know something about karate, but, by conservative estimates, some fifteen million people practice the art. In the long run, however, the karate purest would still find this disturbing. To be more precise and to explain this irritation with concrete examples, I find the following to be particularly out of step with the philosophies of the progenitors of karate and its associated art forms: karate tournaments whose "referees" and sponsors allow and often encourage violence and mayhem (e.g., what was depicted in the final scenes in the movie *The Karate Kid)* in the *kumite* or free-style matches; instructors who award ranks and colored belts for mere hours of practice-time spent, or for so-called business and/or political reasons; instructors whose main concern is financial and charge exorbitant fees, who have infected the art with various degrees of questionable contractual agreements for the payment of same; individuals who involve themselves in petty bickering over the question of who deserves to head local, state, national, and international karate associations, each claiming superiority; those who boisterously emphasize superiority of one style over another; and lastly, those individuals with varying degrees of karate knowledge who train with the secret hope that someday they will have the opportunity to viciously test their acquired skills. This is but a partial list, though it is sufficient to emphasize my point. On a brighter note, we have seen in the last twenty years some successes with efforts to create national and international karate governing organizations. During this same period, martial arts schools have in general improved, though not all favor the students' interests over profit.

Karate has become westernized even to the point of its incorrect pronunciation: (caw-RAH-dee). Karate today is a multi-million dollar business in the United States. With padding and protective headgear, karate contests can now take on the facade of boxing or just plain fighting. So-called "full-contact karate" is a television event in many countries, and there are numerous "world champions." In a sense, some karate *sensei* (teachers) today merely proselytize the art for profit's sake.

The negative aspects of the Asian martial arts are certainly in need of some kind of purification. Perhaps, however, I am coming down too hard on something that is inevitable in any art's progression. When something as popular as karate becomes mainstream, changes are bound to occur, and these changes are not always for the better. There are good karate training gyms extant today, with qualified *sensei* that have high moral reasons for teaching martial arts, instead of merely earning a living. The problem for the neophyte in choosing the correct facility is compounded because he or she really does not know the qualifications of the teacher. With self-promotion in the martial arts rampant today (see Chap. 11), studying with a self-proclaimed ninth- or tenth-degree *sensei* does not guarantee the martial arts trainee that quality and the correct philosophical instruction will be forthcoming.

There is a degree of sadness connected with any art that over the years becomes commercially oriented. It is really too much to hope that karate would retain its pure simplicity by being taught only in Buddhist churches or by nonprofit clubs. The only place where this ethic is still practiced is in Japanese universities and at those American colleges that have initiated clubs and/or university classes in Asian martial arts. Hopefully, the reader will understand my point of view more accurately after finishing this work.

Years ago if you were bullied, you sent for a Charles Atlas workout kit and in a few weeks you were supposed to be able to "beat up" the bully who was bothering you. Countless young men and even some women hoped that karate would magically transform them from "wimp" to "superhero" status. Some did gain skills and confidence; most probably learned the hard way that karate is not a "cure-all" for the downtrodden. An acquaintance of a friend of mine in Los Angeles, who studied karate for several years, did not learn the philosophical side of karate and opted for confrontation instead of caution; in a vicious fight, his nose was bitten off by a street tough. Hopefully, this will remain an isolated instance of this kind of mayhem and karate will continue to develop into the positive force that Gichin Funakoshi dreamed of so long ago in Okinawa and Japan.

I am indebted to a great many people for their cooperation and time spent in interviews and discussions concerning karate and other martial arts. Individual acknowledgment would be impossible; however, special thanks must be given to the following people for help above and beyond that expected or even hoped for: to my daughter Shanna for shooting and developing a number of the photos in this new edition; to Dr. Minoru Shinoda for his patience in guiding me through the rigors of a graduate thesis; to Dr. Benjamin C. Stone at the University of Malaya for his source materials on Malaysian *bersilat*; to Mr. Rudy Ter Linden and Mr. Paul de Thousars, Indonesian fighting experts, who graciously spent hours in demonstrating and speaking of their native combat arts; to Chinei Kinjo, editor of the Okinawan newspaper *Yoen Jiho Sha* in Honolulu, for his time spent on gathering data on Okinawan karate pioneers in Hawaii; to May Choye, Akio Inoue, and James

Umeda, for their hours spent in aiding my translation of Chinese and Japanese sources; to my old instructors, William Chow, Masaichi Oshiro, Kenneth Murakami, and George Miyasaki (I did pay for those cracked seeds!) for their help in teaching me the basics of karate; to *sensei* Tsutomu Ohshima, for his assistance in finding some of the historical karate roots in California; to *eskrimador* Tim Tackett, *hapkido* Master Chong Sung Kim, *hapkido* instructor Jeff Harris, and karate *sensei* Ty Aponte for their information and photographic demonstrations that vividly illustrated their arts; to Robert Young for his input on the Korean martial arts; to Professor Mark Wiley for proofreading the section on the Filipino martial arts and for providing photos of Filipino and Indian martial arts; to the publisher for the illustration that appears on page 116; to officers Henry B. Haina, Jr. and Leon J. Tasor III for posing for the photo on page 159; to Linda Lee for the photo on page 182; and lastly, to Richard White, whose editorial help and suggestions kept me on task in the early years of this work.

Claremont, California

CHAPTER 1

BACKGROUND

IN THE sixth century, China was approaching her zenith as the most "cultured" and powerful nation on earth. China's suzerainty over her immediate neighbors was absolute. She exacted tribute not only from these bordering states, but also from countries hundreds of miles from her periphery, and was thus recognized as the central power of the globe.

As early as the Shang dynasty (*ca.* 1766–1122 B.C.), Arabian camel caravans roamed freely between west-central Asia and China proper, enabling the Middle East, and later the West, to enjoy Chinese products such as silk, tea, porcelain, paper, and gunpowder, the so-called "five great treasures of old Cathay." That these caravans were able to successfully traverse these difficult and often dangerous routes is a tribute to the Arabs' skill and their ability to defend themselves against constant bandit attacks. Their fighting ability was due in no small way to their exposure to both the great powers of the East and of the West, and to their eclectic abilities in borrowing the best of the combat techniques from each.

China did not solicit Western goods. But, as the major power of Asia, she felt obligated to return her satellites' tribute gifts with favors of greater measure and value. Thus far more material wealth left China than was brought in; however, in this process of material exploitation, two unique gifts were to find their way into China that would greatly alter her cultural heritage. Traveling out of India in approximately A.D. 525, an obscure Buddhist monk named Bodhidharma crossed the Chinese frontier[1*] and entered a land already exposed to Theravada and Mahayana doctrines, the two major schools of Buddhist philosophy. This self-appointed religious mission, of seemingly little consequence, is monumental when viewed in its historical perspective. In most of East Asia today, this Indian monk is revered as the spiritual father of Zen Buddhism and the founder of a weaponless fighting art that was the precursor of modern-day karate.

The term "karate" has been widely known in the Western world for little more than forty years. To some, the word has almost a religious connotation; for others it evokes images of physical violence such as the bare-handed breaking of bricks and boards, and combat between man and man or man and beast. But regardless of the viewpoint, the important fact is that karate has become a very real part of Western life and holds the promise of becoming thoroughly integrated into Western culture. Unfortunately, most of those who have, until now, attempted to exploit this

[*] These numbers refer to the Notes that can to be found in the back of the book.

tremendous interest in karate have relied on unauthoritative sources for their information. This is sadly attested to by the many karate students and teachers who, with little or no first-hand knowledge of this art's beginnings and development, freely "explain" it to interested members of the press and television.

Karate is basically an art of unarmed self-defense. In this respect it is similar to judo and sumo wrestling. Its chief point of departure from the others is that karate emphasizes the kick, the open-handed strike, and the closed-fist strike rather than the takedown, the hold, and the throw. So effective is this form of self-defense that it is said a karate master can defend himself against a great number of adversaries, human or animal.

Karate has developed to a high degree of proficiency on Okinawa and Japan and multitudes of karate schools are found throughout these islands. On the Japanese university campus in particular, karate is becoming as traditional as the professorial lecture and the writing of term papers.

Terminology

It is commonly held that karate developed either in Japan proper, or on Okinawa during the time that it was a rather formidable island kingdom. But, careful scrutiny of Asian history reveals overwhelming proof that karate-like arts existed in various parts of Asia long before they were known in either Japan or Okinawa. In the present-day Japanese language the ideographs for karate are 空手 meaning "empty hand" and are pronounced (kah-rah-tay) with equal emphasis on each syllable. Prior to the twentieth century, various terms were used in Chinese and Japanese to describe certain fighting systems that existed on Okinawa and that had marked similarities to modern karate. The Japanese reading of some of these systems are *kempo* 拳法, *tode* 唐手, and *te* 手.[2]

It happens that the term "kempo" means "law of the fist" or "way of the fist" and is read *ch'uan fa* in Mandarin and *ken fat* in Cantonese. It designates a Chinese form of self-defense and self-development very similar to karate. This in itself implies a probable connection between the two forms.

"Tode" is another term suggestive of Chinese influence on karate. The first character, *to* 唐, of *tode* is the symbol for T'ang, the name of the great Chinese dynasty that flourished between A.D. 618–906 and influenced Japan in many ways. In fact, so great was the admiration of the T'ang by Japan that in the centuries that followed the demise of this great dynasty, the character *to,* which is also read as *kara,* was used as an adjective meaning "China." The ideograph combination 唐手 can thus be read either as "tode" or "karate."

Te simply means "hand." However, as early as 1629 this term was used on Okinawa to describe a fighting style that bears a strong resemblance to modern karate.[3]

The use of the ideograph 空 to stand for *kara* is, as we shall see, a twentieth-century development. In 1905 karate was included in the physical education curriculum of Okinawa's intermediate schools. The ideographs 唐手, pronounced (kah-rah-tay), were standard on Okinawa at this time.[4] In 1906 an Okinawan karate master named Chomo Hanagi broke from this traditional way of writing karate and used the other *kara* 空 ideograph for his book, *Karate Soshu Hen.*[5] This work is the first written record in which *kara* is represented by a different written character.

In October, 1936, the Okinawan newspaper *Ryukyu Shimpo Sha* sponsored a meeting of the great Okinawan karate masters Yabu, Kiyamu, Motobu, Miyagi, and Hanagi, in Naha, capital city of Okinawa.[6] The purpose of the meeting was to discuss certain aspects of karate, including the use of the T'ang character in writing karate, and its implications concerning the art.[7] It was decided that the *kara* 空 ideograph was best suited for the writing of the word, both because this ideograph was closely associated with Buddhist philosophy (see Chap. 8, p. 112) and because in dispensing with the *to* 唐 ideograph, they would erase any association with China. The result of this meeting was that by 1937, the 空手 form of writing karate became standardized and has remained unchanged to the present day.[8]

Besides the Okinawan and Chinese prototypes described above, there were five fighting systems that may have contributed to modern-day karate. They were: Egyptian barehanded fighting as depicted in pyramid wall murals; Roman gladiatorial combat; Japanese sumo wrestling; Indian and Persian foot fighting; and a genus of weaponless fighting found in Thailand, Malaysia, Cambodia, Laos, and Vietnam.[9] Even though there is no apparent link between the five techniques, karate contains elements from all of them. The implication, of course, is that karate must have developed in a country that carried on an active and extensive intercourse with the West as well as with all of Asia. The finger of logic points inevitably to China, although India appears to have been the birthplace for some archaic forms of weaponless combat.

印度

CHAPTER 2
INDIA

INDIA HAD traditionally veiled herself in a cloak of pacifism until shortly after Word War II. Mahatma Gandhi's nonviolent struggle for independence from England in the 1930s and 1940s led to the popular belief that India was intrinsically and historically anti-military. This is not an accurate assumption. Warfare was, in fact, an integral part of early Indian culture.

Numerous kingdoms of various sizes dotted the subcontinent in pre-Christian times, each vying with one another for local supremacy. Warfare was thrust upon the people and all types of combat formed a special niche in India's earlier civilizations. A warrior class called the *Kshatriya,* who can best be compared to the Japanese samurai and the medieval knights of Europe, were then the dominant strata in Indian society.

Ghanshyan Jaynagerker demonstrating *Lathi*, an ancient Indian warrior art.

This military group antedates Buddhism and played the leading role in the development of Indian culture until the rise of the Brahmin or priest caste. Despite the difficulty in accurately pinpointing the evolution of a karate-like art at this early date, we shall see that the *Kshatriya* had a direct relationship with at least one early fighting style.

Early Indian Fighting Arts

The first written evidence of an Indian bare-handed fighting art is mentioned in the well-known Buddhist scripture called the *Lotus Sutra.*[1] In Chapter Fourteen an interesting passage is cited where the historic Buddha, speaking to a follower called Manjusri, says, "In the sphere of action and intimacy the bodhisattva dwells in a state of patience . . . he seeks no intimacy with kings, princes . . . nor with heretics

. . . nor with pugilists."[2] As pugilism is the art or practice of fighting with fists, the Buddha's comment seems clearly to indicate that a karate-like art existed before or during the writing of the *Lotus Sutra.*

The Chinese translation of the *Lotus Sutra,* read *Fa Hua San Ch'ing,* is the most widely accredited version in present-day Asia. Here, the aforementioned pugilistic art is called *hsiang ch'a hsiang p'u* 相叉相撲 .[3] The two ideographs 相叉 mean "mutual striking" or "mutual pounding." The other part of the ideographic combination, 相撲 , means so nearly the same thing that the best translation of the whole phrase is simply "mutual striking." This confirms the Sanskrit translation's indication of a weaponless martial art or sporting combat.

The characters 相撲 are also used in Japanese. But there they represent the ancient art of sumo wrestling, a subject to be discussed later (see Chap. 6, p. 96).

Returning to the *Lotus Sutra,* we find reference to another fighting art called *nara* 那羅 .[4] According to one standard Sanskrit-English dictionary the word *nara* means "a manly character; a dancer or performer."[5] Its use is significant because there is a close similarity between Oriental dancing and the martial arts of *ch'uan fa* and karate. *Ch'uan fa,* as was noted previously, is a Chinese style of weaponless fighting closely related to karate. Both of these forms have sets of prescribed exercise and practice movements very similar to shadowboxing in modern pugilism. An untrained observer watching an art similar to *ch'uan fa* for the first time might well believe the practitioner to be dancing. *Nara,* therefore, may not be dancing, but in actuality a fighting style akin to karate or *ch'uan fa.*[6]

Continuing with the proof that a bare-handed fighting art existed in ancient India, we find further reference in an early Buddhist sutra called the *Hongyo-kyo.*[7] Herein is described a "strength contest" between a Prince Nanda and a

Devadatta. Prince Nanda was the half brother of Gautama, the historic Buddha, while Devadatta is thought of as the jealous cousin of the Buddha.[8]

Although we cannot determine with certainty whether this story is fact or myth, the important point for our purpose is that this citation refers to these tests of combat, mentioned frequently in early Indian works. This supports the fact that more than one type of weaponless fighting was extant and was being popularly practiced in India before cropping up in either Chinese or Japanese literature.

Vajramushti and Kalaripayat

India appears to be the birthplace of at lease two more bare-handed fighting arts, *vajramushti* and *kalaripayat*. Evidence seems to indicate that *vajramushti* was the very first karate-like technique and that it was commonly practiced by the *Kshatriya,* or warrior caste. *Vajramushti* is translated as "one whose clenched fist is . . . adamant; of a *Kshatriya,* or warrior; the clenched fist as a weapon."[9]

One modern karate authority, in describing *vajramushti* practice, states that students of this art strengthened their hands by first pouring milk on their fists or by immersing the whole hand into milk, and then striking a slab of marble repeatedly with the knuckles.[10] In India, milk has significance as an object of religious veneration and it is uncertain whether the practice of dipping the fist into milk before striking a punching stone was for religious or medicinal purposes or both.

Most contemporary schools of karate likewise emphasize training of the knuckles by fist striking, some going so far as to use specially prepared Chinese medicines to heal the knuckle skin that inevitably bruises and splits open as a result of overzealous training on the punching board.

Kalaripayat is said to be an ancient karate-like art, and may have been influenced by *vajramushti.*[11]It was practiced in northern India as well as the southern state of Kerala; its dates go back over five thousand years, but it has become known outside of India only recently.[12]

Some weaponry is used in *kalaripayat* along with the weaponless forms; movements are made in conjunction with controlled breathing techniques (*pranayama).*[13] The Northern School of *kalaripayat* was used by descendants of the Nayer people, a fierce warrior caste.[14] It features very high kicking, foot sweeps, and low stances.[15]

It is interesting that some authors associate this art with the style brought to China in the sixth century A.D. by the Indian monk Bodhidharma (see Chap. 3, p. 29).[16] Bodhidharma was carrying the "message" of the historic Buddha and is generally credited with starting the *Ch'an* (Zen) school of Buddhism in China.

Pranayama, the breathing technique of *kalaripayat,* is part of the "Eightfold Path of Discipline" in *Astanga* yoga.[17] It is somewhat perplexing that a discipline of yoga forms an instrumental part of Bodhidharma's *kalaripayat* regimen that was introduced at the Shaolin Temple in the sixth century A.D. Perhaps Bodhidharma was still experimenting with his discipline, which was to become Zen Buddhism. Yoga might be called the "awareness" or "enlightenment" aspect of Hinduism, whereas Zen serves as a similar vehicle in Buddhism. The philosophical aspects of these disciplines are infinitely complex, and Bodhidharma is so historically remote that we may never know the exact origins or philosophical points forming his *kalaripayat.*

It has also been suggested that the Hindu Goddess of Destruction, Kali, was an integral philosophical feature of *kalaripayat.*[18] This further deepens the mystery. Why would Bodhidharma use ritualistic Hindu regimens to spread the Enlightenment School of Buddhism in China?

Historical analysis indicates that he did not use *kalaripayat,* but a form of *vajramushti.* Because of the proximity of Kerala at the southwest tip of India, influence from Southeast Asia would appear likely via the many trade routes that crisscrossed the area.

It is certain that there was some type of weaponless fighting practiced in early Buddhistic India, judging the data that is now available. Mendicant Buddhist monks are said to have utilized both the arts of *hsiang ch'a hsiang p'u* and *vajramushti.*[19] Though the evidence for such an assumption is not abundant, it is interesting to note such an association of a violent martial art with the usually tranquil spirit of Buddhism. This association becomes exceedingly complex as the history of karate unfolds.

One last theory that tends to identify karate with Indian bare-handed fighting is based on the Buddhist statuary of India. Many of the postures of early Indian works have a marked resemblance to karate forms.[20] This applies particularly to the eleven-headed, thousand-armed *Kannon,* which is a Buddhist mythical deity found in many Japanese temples and statues of the so-called *Nio* deities.

These *Nio Bodhisattvas,* replicas of earlier Indian prototypes, are the protectors of the Buddhist faith and are often referred to by the Sanskrit term of *Vira* (or *Vajraprani)* and the Japanese word *Kongorikishi.*[21] A large number of these statues are found as guardians in the gate entrances to Buddhist temples, usually in an exact karate stance.

Although none of the foregoing bits of evidence can be considered conclusive proof that a form of karate existed in ancient India, taken as a whole they point so overwhelmingly to such a conclusion that it is impossible to think otherwise. As we shall now see, this germinal idea was taken into China and nurtured into an empty-handed fighting art so formidable that its exponents were referred to with a reverential air.

CHAPTER 3
CHINA

CHINA, LIKE India, has been the nurturing spot for numerous martial art forms. While some of these arts were actually initiated in China, many were brought in from other countries and so Sinicized after centuries of practice in China that today they appear to be of Chinese inspiration.

It is difficult, even with access to reams of statistical data to determine bases or patterns for behavior, and the task is enormously amplified when the behavioral patterns were established hundreds of years in the past. For this reason, it cannot be authoritatively determined why the earliest *ch'uan fa* schools were so secretive that it was considered a capital offense to display the techniques to the uninitiated. This particular behavior pattern has made extremely difficult the task of the historian studying Chinese weaponless martial arts.

In the field of weaponless combat, China undoubtedly was the catalyst in producing the techniques that have eventually come to be called karate. While the major Chinese precursor of karate is *ch'uan fa* in Mandarin Chinese, it is more popularly known as kung fu 功夫 (pronounced "gung-foo"). Although we call *ch'uan fa* a Chinese art, it is doubtful that it is wholly a product of Chinese genius.

We know, for example, that from India's influence on China there arose at least one form of bare-handed fighting, the pioneer of which was the Indian monk, Bodhidharma.

Bodhidharma and the Shaolin Temple

Bodhidharma is an obscure figure in history. The most reliable sources for our knowledge of the man are generally considered to be *Biographies of the High Priests* by Priest Tao-hsuan, written in A.D. 654, and the *Records of the Transmission of the Lamp,* by Priest Tao-yuan, written in 1004.[1] But the earliest written source concerning Bodhidharma is found in a work entitled *Records of the Lo-yang Temple,* by Yang Hsuan Chih in 547.[2] These seemingly authentic sources notwithstanding, however, modern scholarship has been either reluctant to accept any single version of Bodhidharma's existence, or it asserts that all accounts of the Indian monk are legendary (see Paul Pelliot in *T'oung Pao,* 1923). On the other hand, eminent Buddhist-historians such as D. T. Suzuki, Kenneth Ch'en, and Heinrich Dumoulin, feel that Bodhidharma was an actual person despite the many admitted sprinklings and spicings of myth that have been added to his biography.

Bodhidharma was the third child of King Sugandha in southern India,[3] was a member of the *Kshatriya,* or warrior caste,[4] and had his childhood in Conjeeveram[5] (also, Kanchipuram, Kancheepuram), the small but dynamically Buddhist province south of Madras. He is said to have received his religious training from the *Dhyana* master Prajnatara, who was responsible for changing the young disciple's name from Bodhitara.[6] An apt pupil, Bodhidharma soon exceeded his contemporaries so that by the time of his middle age, he was considered to be very wise in the ways of *Dhyana,* or Zen practices. When Prajnatara died, Bodhidharma set sail for China, possibly because of a deathbed wish from his old master, according to the *Records of Lo-yang Temple.*[7] On the other hand, Tao-yuan's *Records of the Transmission of the Lamp* indicate that the decision to go to China was made by Bodhidharma alone, because he was saddened by the decline of Buddhism in the areas outside of India proper.[8]

Accounts of Bodhidharma's activities in China vary considerably with the reference cited. Tao-hsuan's *Biographies of the High Priests* states that Bodhidharma first arrived in China during the Sung dynasty (420–479) of the Southern Dynasties (420–589), and later traveled north to the Kingdom of Wei.[9] But the traditional date of Bodhidharma's entry into China has been 520 (*vars.,* 526, 527). This appears to be rather late if Tao-hsuan's *Biographies . . .* is accurate in placing him at the Yung Ning Temple at Lo-Yang in 520.[10] *Biographies . . .* further states that a Buddhist "novice" called Seng-fu joined Bodhidharma's following, was ordained by Bodhidharma after an undisclosed period of study, and then left to journey to south China where he passed away in 524 at the age of sixty-one.[11] Basic mathematics tells us that if Seng-fu were, indeed, sixty-one in 524, and had been the minimum acceptable age for ordination (twenty years old at that time) when so honored by

Bodhidharma, he would have been twenty in *ca.* 483, putting the Indian monk in China considerably earlier than the traditional date of 520.[12]

A variation of the above theory, found in the *Records of the Transmission of the Lamp* (1004), places Bodhidharma in Canton in 527. After some time there, he traveled northward, meeting the Emperor Wu of the Liang dynasty (502–557) at Chin-ling (now Nanking).[13] It was at this time that the now-famous question-and-answer dialogue took place between the learned monk and Emperor Wu. Realizing that his form of *Dhyana* "questioning" was of little avail with the pious but worldly monarch, Bodhidharma left the court for the Shaolin Monastery,[14] where significant events then took place.

Bodhidharma's meeting with Emperor Liang Wu appears neither in the *Records of the Lo-yang Temple* nor in the *Biographies* . . . ,[15] written in 547 and 654 respectively. Since the *Records of the Transmission of the Lamp* was compiled 350 years after the *Biographies* . . . , when Zen practices had already been well established in China, it is possible that the Bodhidharma-Emperor Wu debate was invented as a reverent allegory for explaining specific Zen tenets. Again there are insufficient historical correlations to enable us to draw a firmly based conclusion.

After the famous but historically questionable encounter between Bodhidharma and Emperor Wu, Bodhidharma's life is centered around the Shaolin Temple and Monastery located in Honan Province. Tradition states that upon seeing the emaciated condition of the monks of this temple, Bodhidharma instructed them in physical exercises to condition their bodies as well as their minds.[16]

In several works dealing with *ch'uan fa* and its Okinawan counterpart, karate, reference is made to the close tie between Bodhidharma's Shaolin exercises and the above-named fighting arts. The factual basis for these hypotheses is the physical drills Bodhidharma introduced to the Shaolin monks, called *Shihpa Lohan Shou,*[17] or in English, "Eighteen Hands of the *Lohan.*"

At the present time *Lohan is* used to designate all famous disciples of the historic Buddha, but more generally the term refers to those five hundred *arhats* (Sanskrit term for those who have achieved nirvana) who are supposed to reappear on earth as Buddhas,[18] according to Buddhist mythology in some sects of the religion.

The precise meaning of *Lohan* in Bodhidharma's time, however, is lost, and we are forced to rely on the educated assumption that they were some form of temple guardians of Hindu origin.[19] It also appears that their original Hindu number was sixteen, and that the Chinese added two to bring the total to eighteen.[20]

According to E.T.C. Werner in his monumental *Dictionary of Chinese Mythology,* there does not appear to be any historical account of the first introduction of the *Lohan* into the halls of Buddhist temples. Werner goes on to state that the Eighteen *Lohan* did not exist before the time of Buddhist poet and artist Kuan-hsiu (832–912). However, we have already seen that martial arts tradition states that the *Shihpa Lohan Shou* were introduced at the Shaolin Monastery sometime after 520, thus designating Bodhidharma as the initiator of the term "Lohan" in Chinese.

For our purposes, however, the main significance of the *Shihpa Lohan Shou,* via Bodhidharma, is that it is reputed to be the basis for the famous Shaolin *ch'uan fa.*[21]

This theory, on the other hand, raises a number of questions. For example, Bodhidharma's chief concern was apparently to cultivate the minds of his followers so that enlightenment could be achieved. Why would a Zen patriarch conceive a form of *ch'uan fa* that, at least in its present stage of evolution, is a brutally effective weapon of combat? The answer, most probably, is that Bodhidharma never intended his *Shihpa Lohan Shou* to be a violent martial art. There is certainly nothing to be found in the Bodhidharma image, as portrayed in the existing references, that would connect him with the later slapping, striking, punching, grunting, and generally violent masters of Zen Buddhism.

Here is an interesting hypothesis that has been overlooked by historians to date. The term traditionally applied to Bodhidharma—"wall-gazing Brahmin"—is a misnomer. Reliable accounts (e.g., Chou's A *History of Chinese Buddhism,* Werner's *Dictionary of Chinese Mythology,* etc.) show that Bodhidharma was a member of the *Kshatriya* or warrior caste in India. As such, he was exposed to all existing forms of weaponless fighting from boyhood. The *Kshatriya*'s most notable bare-handed fighting style was called *vajramushti,* which was described in Chapter 2. Mendicant Buddhist monks as well as the *Kshatriya* are said to have utilized *vajramushti* techniques,[22] and there is little doubt that as a *Kshatriya* in India and later a peripatetic monk in China, Bodhidharma learned this technique of fighting. Whether the *Shihpa Lohan Shou* is specifically an extension of *vajramushti* forms will probably never be known, since little has been written about the development of *vajramushti* per se, and references linking Bodhidharma with "self-defense" techniques are scarce. Tao-hsuan's *Biographies of the High Priests* (654) fails to mention Bodhidharma in connection with anything that could be linked to martial arts. Of course, this omission does not mean that Bodhidharma did not introduce the Shaolin monks to some unique physical and perhaps martial art, especially since few academicians have taken an active interest in the mundane martial arts associated with historical events, and several of the most careful historians who have reputations for accuracy in defining "things Oriental" have "missed the boat," so to speak, when classifying all Asian combat forms as simply "boxing" or "pugilism."

The development of the Shaolin style of unarmed self-defense, though popularly associated with Bodhidharma, has a varied history, again depending on the source. The most plausible version indicates that after Bodhidharma left the monastery, many of the other monks of the Shaolin set out to disseminate his teachings. Contrary to the belief of D.T. Suzuki and others, the martial arts tradition that surrounds Bodhidharma attributed two books to his genius that were found a short while after his demise, secreted in the walls of the temple.[23]

The first work, entitled *Hsi Sui Chin,* was said to have been transcribed by Bodhidharma's disciple Hui K'o[24] and has since been lost to the world. The second work, *I Chin Ching,* has been translated several times and clouding this work is the possibility that it is a forgery from a period well after Bodhidharma's death. Tradition has it that these writings are not only filled with the spirit of Zen Buddhism, but that they also reveal Bodhidharma's position on physical activity as a means of body hygienics. The dubious nature of these writings, however, makes them unacceptable as conclusive historical documents.

Several decades after the death of Bodhidharma a certain *ch'uan fa* master named Ch'ueh Yuan Shang-jen verified the existence of Bodhidharma's "Eighteen Hands of the *Lohan*" exercise and combined these movements with numerous forms of his own style.[25] The obscurity surrounding the life of Ch'ueh Yuan Shang-jen is no less than that which is present in nearly every work dealing with *ch'uan fa.* The existing biographical data on him tells us little more than that he came from either Honan or Shantung Province. But our interest in him is not in his biography but in the fact that he is credited with increasing Bodhidharma's original eighteen hand-and-foot positions to seventy-two.[26]

After Ch'ueh had spent some time popularizing his expanded version of the Shaolin *ch'uan fa,* he traveled to

Shensi Province where he met with another martial arts master named Li-shao. Ch'ueh and Li are said to have enlarged the seventy-two strokes to 170, and to have given the best of these movements such names as dragon, tiger, snake, and crane.

The authoritative French source *La Médecine Chinoise Au Cours Des Siècles* refers to the previously mentioned Ch'ueh Yuan Shang-jen as Kiao Yuan, claiming that it was he who initiated the additional movements to the *Shihpa Lohan Shou* (up to 173 movements) and gave to it a decalog of moral precepts. Whether Ch'ueh Yuan and Kiao Yuan are one and the same is not known, as the romanization of the two surnames gives the same pronunciation. At any rate, it was Ch'ueh Yuan (or Kiao Yuan) who was responsible for the rise and fame of the Shaolin *ch'uan fa*,[27] and therein is where our interest lies.

Most *ch'uan fa* forms practiced in the twentieth century are descendants of the 170 (*var.* 173) hand-and-foot positions of Ch'ueh Yuan, and though they have undergone a steady evolution they can still be traced ultimately to Bodhidharma's embryonic eighteen positions. Yet one more historical episode exists that clouds even this well-authenticated conclusion. During the Sui dynasty (589–618), brigands attacked the Shaolin Monastery.[28] Various futile attempts were made by the resident monks to protect themselves until at last one priest called the "begging monk" drove off the outlaws with a virtuosity of kicking and punching techniques. This performance so impressed the other monks that they asked the "begging monk" to instruct them in his fighting form, which later developed into the famous Shaolin *ch'uan fa*.

Since the popular version in Japan and most of Asia claims that it was Bodhidharma who founded the Shaolin *ch'uan fa*, some readers may mistakenly associate the "begging monk" with Bodhidharma. This assumption is immediately ruled out, however, when we see that the "begging monk" lived during the Sui dynasty, which began in A.D. 589, and well after Bodhidharma's death (*ca.* 534). Hence, the account of the so-called "begging monk" seems to represent a conflicting version of the founding of the Shaolin *ch'uan fa.*

Regardless of one's motives in favoring one account over the other, there are too many references in favor of the Bodhidharma legend to make other narratives truly convincing. In all probability, this spiritual pioneer of Zen in China can be credited with the founding of at least one of the Shaolin styles of *ch'uan fa.* But, as the major task of revising Bodhidharma's original eighteen-stroke exercise to 170 offensive and defensive movements belongs to the previously cited *ch'uan fa* master, Ch'ueh Yuan Shang-jen, we deduce that *ch'uan fa,* as a truly lethal military art, developed with this man.

External and Internal Martial Arts

The Shaolin *ch'uan fa is* the first school of bare-handed fighting listed under the general heading of "External School" or *Wai Chia* 外家.[29] The "External School" is the major classification under which eight other styles are grouped.[30] The exact date of origin for this terminology is not known. It was probably used at first to categorize various types of *ch'uan fa* under one heading after the Shaolin styles came into existence.

The other eight forms listed under the "External School" are *Hung Ch'uan* and *Tau T'ei Yu T'an T'ui* both from the Southern Sung dynasty (A.D. 1127–1279); the *Hon Ch'uan, Erh Lang Men, Fan Ch'uan,* and *Ch'a Ch'uan* styles dated from the Ming dynasty (A.D. 1368–1644)—the latter form used exclusively by Chinese Moslems; and two styles attributed to the Ch'ing dynasty (A.D. 1644–1911), called *Mi Tsung Yi* and *Pa Ch'uan.*[31]

In nearly every instance, the founders of these eight *ch'uan fa* styles were said to have been Taoist deities or demigods. The real creators of these various forms appear to be lost to the world and, as the so-called godlike inventors are timeless entities in the mythology of China, many Chinese believe that *ch'uan fa* has always existed. Historically dating the first public display of the above-named styles of *ch'uan fa* has thus far been impossible. The importance of the *ch'uan fa*-Taoist association will be discussed later (Chap. 8, p. 118).

The same obscurity found in the history of the "External School" is likewise seen in the background of the "Internal School" of *ch'uan fa,* called *Nei Chia* 内家. These forms are all from the Sung or post-Sung period and are called: *Wu Tang P'ai, T'ai Ch'i Ch'uan, Pa Kua Ch'uan, Hsing I Ch'uan, Tzu Jan Men,* and *Liu He Pa Fa.*[32]

Bodhidharma's final days are shrouded in the mystery of marvelous and supernatural events. After transmitting the "dharma" to his disciple Hui K'o at the Shaolin Temple, one version has it that he died and was neatly and properly buried on Hsiung-erh Shan (Bear's Ear Hill),[33] in Honan Province. Those who ascribe to this "neat and proper" theory vary in his death date between 529 and 535.[34] However, we then encounter a work entitled *Shen Hsien T'ung Chien,*[35] wherein a Wei official en route to Central Asia for a goodwill mission reported a cordial meeting with Bodhidharma at Ch'ung-lin (Onion Range) in the Belaturgh Mountains of Turkestan. Carrying a single sandal, Bodhidharma was asked by the official where he was going, to which the monk replied: "I am going back to the Western Heaven (India)."[36]

This tale was later reported to the Wei Emperor who accordingly exhumed Bodhidharma's tomb, wherein he found . . . one sandal.[37] The emperor, awed by this "resurrection," attempted to preserve the surviving foot garment in the Shaolin Monastery, but even it disappeared (reportedly stolen) before the passage of two centuries.[38]

Bodhidharma's final exit in Chinese history under such strange circumstances is certainly in character with the general mode of sixth-century Chinese thought. Mysticism, magic, and supernatural entities were the "stuff" of which early Chinese folklore, and post-first-century Buddhist religious thought, were made.

There is every possibility that some type of weaponless combat developed in China long before the advent of Bodhidharma. According to one authority, a certain form of *ch'uan fa* evolved in China approximately five thousand years ago during the reign of the semimythical Yellow Emperor, Huang-ti.[39]

There is further reference to the birth of this art in the dynastic history known as the *Han Shu* (Western Han dynasty 206 B.C.–A.D. 24), but the date ascribed to it is much too remote in antiquity to be convincing. Thus, other than saying that something akin to *ch'uan fa*-karate developed very early in China, we can make no definitive statements about its beginning.

Secret Societies and the Chinese Martial Arts

Secret societies have played an important role in Chinese history from earliest times; however, the first outspokenly antigovernment group existed near the end of the Han dynasty, called the "Carnation Eyebrow Rebels."[40] Because of the effectiveness of this society in accomplishing its aims, the list of such organizations grew until eventually wherever political oppression became intolerable, or a foreign power came to rule (such as the Mongols of Marco Polo's

Wong Ark Yuey showing a *ch'uan fa* salute. Similar hand signs were used by anti-Manchu rebels to identify themselves.

time), these secret societies led the fight in restoring locally desirable government.

From 1644 a foreign Manchu dynasty controlled China's destiny, subjecting the multitudes of Chinese to the role of second-class citizens. Agitation for reform and overthrow of the Manchu autocracy brought swift reprisals to participants therein. So, to end this government oppression, Chinese secret societies went "underground" and became the leading protagonists for anti-Manchu activity.

The Ch'ing dynasty (1644–1911) of the Manchus thus became a leading target for revolutionary activities of various groups, with the famous and powerful "White Lotus Society" heading the attempted coup that included such secret anti-Manchu groups as the "Three Incense Sticks," "The Rationalist Society," and the "Eight Diagrams."[41]

In the middle of the nineteenth century, Western powers began their long-anticipated economic and military assault on the Middle Kingdom. A beleaguered China, proud of her ancient civilization and scornful of the Occidental "barbarians," was unsuccessful in forestalling European aggression and final victory. England led the way in opening China's sealed doors, forcing her to war in 1839 and 1856, with the French joining the British in the latter encounter. These involvements cost China the island of Hong Kong, which was ceded to the British for war reparations, as well as numerous "treaty ports" on the Chinese mainland, not to mention various other "rights" and advantages including the right to freely import opium.

Western imperialism was at first only a minor irritation to the general mass of Chinese people for whom foreign invasion was an expected part of life. In the past millennia of Chinese history the transgressors had eventually left China of their own accord or, being Mongoloid peoples, they were assimilated into the Chinese culture and not thought of as invaders. The foreign Manchus, though in control of China for nearly three hundred years, had been oppressive rulers and Chinese hatred was centered on the Manchu dynasty. However, after the Opium War of 1839, England and all other foreign "barbarians" slowly became the objects of Chinese animosity. After a time the United States joined additional European nations in obtaining similar guarantees in China.[42] By the beginning of the twentieth century Chinese sovereignty had virtually ceased to exist.

Hatred of Western domination reached a breaking point in 1900 when the Boxers staged their famous rebellion. The significance of this revolt for our purposes lies in the fact that the Boxers were involved in a type of *ch'uan fa* activity.

The term "Boxers" was first applied to *ch'uan fa* cultists by Westerners in China when they saw a similarity between *ch'uan fa* and their own brands of pugilistic encounter. And, although very few *ch'uan fa* schools seem to have participated in the Boxer Rebellion, they became lumped together under the term "Boxers," which eventually was used by the invading Westerners to indicate any Chinese secret society or group that demonstrated hatred of the West. One large group of Boxers, and it seems that this society was more responsible for the term "Boxers" than any other, was called the *I-Ho-Ch'uan* or "Righteous and Harmonious Fists," of which only a small portion were *ch'uan fa* practitioners. The *I-Ho-Ch'uan* was a branch of an older secret organization, the aforementioned "Eight Diagrams," founded near the close of the Ming dynasty. This "Eight Diagrams" was probably not a *ch'uan fa* association either, but affiliated with it were certain *ch'uan fa* groups such as the *I-Ho-Ch'uan*. The "Eight Diagrams" society became a leading anti-Western clique before and during the short Boxer war of 1900.[43]

Two other Boxer groups that may have had strong *ch'uan*

fa membership were the *K'an* and *Ch'ien* Boxers.[44] These two groups were active in northern China during the 1900 rebellion and were associated with both the *I-Ho-Ch'uan* and the "Eight Diagrams."[45] Besides the more clandestine activities of the various secret societies, the 1900 war also attracted multitudes of Chinese men, both young and old, who formed into bands of "gymnasts"[46] and who practiced numerous forms of *ch'uan fa.*

In retrospect, the Boxer Rebellion was an unorganized mass revolt against foreign controls in China. The amount of actual *ch'uan fa* activity was slight, although the ruling Manchu aristocracy and the peasantry seemed to have been mesmerized by *ch'uan fa* performers into believing that they could outdo the mighty Western military science with their weaponless art. It is interesting to note that the appeal of *ch'uan fa* was sufficient to enlist the masses in this revolt against the foreign elements, in spite of the knowledge that their opponents would be retaliating with every type of firearm in their possession. As it turned out, most of the actual combat during the rebellion was conducted with weapons. The empty-handed or true *ch'uan fa* styles seem to have been employed primarily for propaganda purposes.

For two months, from June 20 to August 14 (1900), the Kansu Army of Tung Fu Hsing and hundreds of 'righteous' people flourished all sorts of magic weapons such as soul-absorbing banners, sky-covering flags, thunderbolt fans, and flying swords. They succeeded in killing only one important person, the German Minister Von Ketteler.[47]

Wushu in the People's Republic of China

Throughout history, China probably had the most secretive forms of martial arts. We have seen how secret societies flourished in Chinese history; how absolute secrecy was necessary for survival, and how martial arts were an integral part of these clandestine organizations. This was to be the norm well into the second half of the twentieth century.

The most prominent term used for Chinese martial arts today is *wushu*. This term means "art of war," (*bu-jutsu* in Japanese) and is used to describe over four hundred schools and styles.[48] Before the 1980s, kung fu was more commonly used in the West to describe these same arts, and being a Cantonese word, is still prevalent where southern Chinese predominate.

In every true art form, whether aesthetic or practical, some part of the artist's technique is kept secret. This was especially true of the Chinese martial arts until the 1960s. Before this decade, Chinese martial arts were displayed only in Chinese New Year's parades and celebrations, mostly by children and young adults representing cultural and provincial societies. Chapter 9 will deal with the initial "open" Chinese martial arts classes (i.e., no race restrictions) that developed in the United States.

The twentieth century, far from witnessing the demise of *wushu*, has seen a great rise in its popularity. In Communist China, Mao Tse-tung utilized the appeal of *wushu* to enlist participants in his gymnastic program, as well as for a pragmatic form of self-defense that everyone was urged to learn. However, not knowing exactly what might happen to practitioners of traditional arts, many of China's top *wushu* instructors fled to Taiwan and Hong Kong.[49] These instructors were lucky to escape the Cultural Revolution of the mid-1960s and the reactionary treatment of things considered old fashioned and traditional. Even the venerable Shaolin Temple had carvings and other art objects destroyed.

Interestingly, today in the 1990s, the Shaolin Monastery has been nearly restored and is a fully operational religious order and martial arts training center, seeing up to sixty thousand tourists daily![50] There is even a biennial International Shaolin *Wushu* Festival that in 1991 attracted thirty-seven delegations from twenty-two different countries.[51]

Today, over fifty countries are members of the International *Wushu* Federation (IWF), including the United States, which joined August 21, 1993.[52] China was the site of the first World *Wushu* Championship in 1991, and Malaysia in 1993.

Far from training in Chinese organizations exclusively, the Chinese martial arts are "out of the closet" so to speak and readily available to any and all who wish to study and train. This is certainly a far cry from the author's days in Honolulu in the 1950s when kung fu was strictly for those with Chinese surnames.

CHAPTER 4 SOUTHEAST ASIA

東南亞

MARTIAL ART development is largely based on imitation followed by periods and degrees of refinement. That is, most newly forming societies look to countries with an already-established system of fighting for guidance in developing their own military organizations. Few peoples have been inventive enough to develop original concepts of combat, especially in the realm of empty-handed fighting. Thus, as weaponless martial arts systems have long existed in Southeast Asia, the problem of where, when, and how they evolved becomes very important to the martial arts historian.

Southeast Asia is at the same time a land of fabled romance, myth, and legend, and one of monotonous sameness. Blessed with abundant natural resources, it is a land where the people of many diverse cultures generally have lived easily from the earth's abundance, seldom experiencing the tragedy of starvation as did their nearby East Asian neighbors. The patterns of life are generally unhurried and simple, and have been little affected by the vagaries of world political struggles until very recently, though the arm of colonial tyranny did reach out to choke off the initiative of the native peoples in many areas of Southeast Asia as early as the sixteenth century.

Such comparative self-sufficiency, coupled with the tropical languor so often found among peoples living in the earth's torrid regions, should probably have sufficed to prevent the development of serious fighting arts, since they demand such extremes of effort and self-discipline. However, as Southeast Asia had in ages past been the site of several magnificent civilizations, it did spawn numerous aesthetic and practical arts that are in every way equal to those developed by her East Asian neighbors—China, Korea, and Japan.

Only recently have students of Asian history "discovered" that empty-handed self-defense techniques have existed in Southeast Asia for hundreds of years. This is because they have been able to find so little written on the subject, and have thus had to rely on interviews with natives who are usually quite reluctant to speak about their arts. In fact, until archaeological expeditions hacked their way through the forbidding jungles and discovered structure after magnificent structure of former highly developed civilizations, there was no evidence whatsoever that verified the fact that such arts had been a part of Southeast Asian history. But slowly, after sifting carefully through the potpourri of wall carvings, temple friezes, and religious and secular statuary that so richly adorn these remains, the story of empty-handed martial art development has presented itself to those willing to investigate the record in stone.

Logically, we should approach the problem from two standpoints: First, from a consideration of the forms that are thought to be indigenous to Southeast Asia; and second, through an investigation of the styles that appear to be imported from outside of this geographic area.

Cambodia

Present-day Cambodia stands at the site where the famed Khmer Empire once flourished. For over six hundred years (A.D. 802–1432) the Khmers dominated much of Southeast Asia.[1] This great empire is said to have been the end result of a centuries-long migration of adventure-seeking "pioneers" from far-away India,[2] where imaginations had been inflamed by traders' stories of the immense wealth and unbelievable beauty of the "Land far to the East." As their isolation from "Mother India" grew more pronounced through the years, these people developed a unique culture of their own. But because of the never-ceasing influx of Indian scholars and priests, the Khmer and the Indian were never entirely divorced.

A series of strong Khmer rulers restlessly expanded their territory, gathering the land's abundant fruits into an ever-burgeoning stockpile of riches, until soon the Khmer capital was recognized as one of the great cultural centers of Southeast Asia. Probably the most magnificent structures erected during this period were Suryavarman II's awe-inspiring temple of Angkor Wat, Jayavarman VII's walled city of Angkor Thom, and the strikingly detailed Bayon Temple.[3] It is in, on, and around the ruins of these now-decaying structures that a series of statues and animated reliefs are found depicting various phases of weaponless fighting.[4] In fact, figures portrayed in some form of close combat number in the thousands,[5] among which are many in fighting stances that are unmistakably from Chinese *ch'uan fa.*

The story that these statues tell is one of pronounced Chinese influence in early Southeast Asian history. This fact is well substantiated when we realize that it is from Chinese writings that most of our knowledge of the early Khmer comes, and that many of these writings are dated at the beginning of the Christian era.[6] A fascinating tale of peaceful exchange and interplay between two great kingdoms has unfolded from fragments pieced together only recently. Although we will not delve into it too deeply, suffice it to say that the earliest Khmer Kingdom, called Funan (A.D. 100–600), was visited regularly by Chinese traders and diplomatic envoys. That a very pronounced cultural exchange took place is attested to by Funan's sending a troop of Khmer musicians and dancers to entertain the Emperor of China in the third century.[7] These and other written facts offer the strong suggestion that many elements of early Khmer weaponless fighting were inspired by Chinese forms.

The early Indian arts of *hsiang ch'a hsiang p'u, nara, kalaripayat* and *vajramushti* seem to have no visual representation in Southeast Asia. By that we mean that no archaeological findings have yet indicated that these ancient Indian forms were introduced into Cambodia or elsewhere on the continental portion of Asia known geographically as "Southeast Asia." Thus although we know that there was a certain amount of intercourse between early India and Southeast Asia, we have no tangible evidence that early Khmer styles of fighting were descendents of any or all of the four above-cited Indian forms. And yet, since Indian ideas and practices flowed almost continuously into the Khmer Kingdom during the first millennium of the Khmer civilization,[8] it seems probable that India had a pronounced influence on the development of Khmer unarmed fighting. However, any conclusion based on the scanty evidence available would be historically hazardous.

The notion that many of the carvings and statues found in some form of unarmed fighting portray an original Khmer concept of bare-handed combat seems to be a logical deduction from the following fact: man has always used fists for weapons. The use of "hands" for fighting is seen even in highly evolved animals such as the kangaroo, bear, the big cats, and all of the primates. Boxing as a refined skill had its beginnings over twenty-five hundred years ago, as attested to by its inclusion in the Twenty-Third Olympiad in Greece (688 B.C.).[9] It became such a popular sport that it rather quickly reached a high level of development. Because of the naturalness with which such combat comes to man, it is reasonable to assume that the Khmers did devise their own form of bare-handed fighting. Thus the best assumption is that Khmer bare-handed fighting borrowed from both China and India, and gave to each in turn, but remained throughout a unique style unto itself.

Vietnam

The name "Vietnam" today conjures up horrible images of slaughter and war. The Vietnam War brought on suffering to millions of people in the former French Colony of Indochina and the U.S., and destruction surpassed only by World War II. The psychological trauma goes on. However, to the martial artist, Vietnam is another link in the chain of Asian martial arts akin to karate.

Historically, this small, narrow country has had the dubious distinction of being the only Southeast Asian country under nearly constant Chinese subjugation for the past two thousand years.[10] The founding of the kingdom called

"Nam-Viet" occurred in 208 B.C. and was composed of parts of present-day China and Northern Vietnam.[11] This kingdom, though independent in name, gave allegiance to the Han emperors of China.[12] Then, during one of China's expansion programs in 111 B.C., it was annexed and became an official part of the Middle Kingdom.

Ch'uan fa was practiced in Vietnam throughout written history, a fact recognized in the numerous Chinese martial arts schools extant there. However, recently so-called traditional Vietnamese styles have also surfaced.

Chau Quan Khi is the Vietnamese name of a Chinese Shaolin *ch'uan fa* master from Canton, China. He entered Vietnam in the late 1930s where he founded a Vietnamese martial arts school in 1956.[13] This Vietnamese style was undoubtedly influenced to some degree by his Shaolin training. Chau became a naturalized citizen of the then-French colony and named Pham Xuan Tong as his successor.[14]

Pham took up residence in France in 1968. In the early 1980s he created a new martial art known as *Quankido*.[15] Some call this a "new" art; however, its roots show the eclectic character of many, if not most, Asian martial arts. *Quankido* is similar to karate but more acrobatic and spectacular; Vietnamese weapons such as the sword are also utilized.[16] France has over three thousand members in about one hundred *Quankido* clubs.[17]

In 1945, a Vietnamese master named Nguyen Loc opened a "traditional" Vietnamese martial arts school in Hanoi. He is credited with creating several Vietnamese styles, namely *Vovinam Viet Vo Dao* and *Viet Vo Dao*.[18]

Cholon, the Chinese section of Ho Chi Minh City (formerly Saigon), boasts a large ethnic Chinese population that still practices many styles of traditional Chinese *ch'uan fa*.[19]

A certain amount of Japanese influence in other areas of

unarmed and armed combat took place during the Japanese occupation of Indochina during World War II. This is interesting because although there is seldom a great deal of cultural exchange between victor and vanquished, there are always certain men who vigorously pursue new and untried physical activities that they feel will contribute to their self-improvement.

Judo is one such example. In the days of the Republic of Vietnam (1955–1975), judo was popular. The largest *dojo* in Saigon was, during most of the day, a wild scene of white-garbed judoka grappling and straining for victory under the watchful eyes of the founder of judo, Jigoro Kano, whose portrait was prominently displayed on the wall. Though judo is a Japanese art, the Vietnamese call it by their own term, *nhu dao*, which like judo, translates as "gentle way."[20]

Little more can be said about fighting arts in Vietnam. This will certainly change in the years ahead as the United States and the Democratic Republic of Vietnam move closer to formal diplomatic ties. There are already several Vietnamese martial arts schools in Southern California that are accepting non-Vietnamese into their ranks. This will definitely produce more insight into these rather obscure arts.

Thailand

Thai kingdoms and Thai military ventures have for centuries played an instrumental role in the history of Southeast Asia. It was a warring Thai state that brought disaster to the Khmer Empire in 1432, and that, through the following centuries, dominated the area from Singapore to the Chinese border, and from the mouth of the Irrawaddy to the lower Mekong River.[21]

Numerous forms of unarmed combat are found in modern Thailand, the most famous—or notorious—of which is simply called "Thai boxing" (*Muay Thai*). The precursor to this form was an ancient martial art called *mai si sok* and was not a sport but a form of life-and-death hand-to-hand combat.[22] The more successful techniques of *mai si sok* were handed down and called *pahu yuth*. When the name of the country was changed from Siam to Thailand, this fighting art became known as *Muay Thai*.[23]

The metamorphosis of this fighting art into a sport occurred in the late 1930s. Because *Muay Thai* originally used horsehide thongs wrapped around the fists and tree bark or hollowed-out coconuts as groin protectors, injuries were frequent and serious. A certain Ajan Jua Jaksuraksa set up the *Muay Thai* boxing rules to conform to international standards, under which padded boxing gloves were worn and weight divisions were used. Today, tourists as well as Thai citizens can be found thronging to the many fighting arenas in and around the capital city of Bangkok or watching the almost nightly bouts on television. To the uninitiated, a Thai boxing contest first appears to be classically Western; the participants wear boxing gloves and trunks, and square off in a roped fighting ring. However, when the contest begins, those of us who are accustomed to "Marquis of Queensberry" rules are immediately shocked by the combatants' sudden lighting-like kicks to their opponents' legs, torso, and head, or swift knees and elbow strikes, all of which are allowable under Thai boxing rules.

Some have stated that the rite or dancelike invocation performed by both fighters before the match is so typically Indian in character that one almost expects to hear the chanting of verses from the *Ramayana* or to witness the execution of an Indian play. This prefight ritual is, however, Thai in every aspect and is called the *wai kru*. It is a warm-up for the contestants, a prayer to avoid injury, and way to pay homage to one's teacher.[24] The *wai kru* is accompanied by flutes, drums, and cymbals and varies from one *Muay Thai* camp to another.

The combat itself is remindful of other Southeast Asian kicking styles and has prompted more than one writer to speculate that it was the precursor of Okinawan karate. The famous actor and martial artist, Bruce Lee, strongly endorsed *Muay Thai* techniques.

Thai boxing made some fleeting appearances on American television in the early 1970s. It was shown because of its violence and "exotic" nature. These bouts were fought in Japan, promoted by Japanese television, and later shown in America.[25] Because half of these bouts were lost by Thai fighters, there was an outcry in Thailand and some of the Thais later admitted they took bribes to lose their matches.[26] According to Thai sources, in most instances where *Muay Thai* fighters were matched against judoka, karateka, kung fu stylists, etc., the non-Thai fighters proved to be no match. These same Thai sources chronicle a number of famous matches between *Muay Thai* fighters and assorted other fighting stylists dating from the sixteenth century A.D. to modern times. *Muay Thai* was the victorious style in over ninety percent of the contests.

The brief appearance of *Muay Thai* in the United States brought about a new revolution in the Asian martial arts, e.g. kickboxing and full-contact karate. Joe Lewis, a Shorin-ryu stylist, is reputed to have introduced full-contact karate in 1970.[27] Lewis went on to fight in full-contact events during the 1970s. Another American influenced by *Muay Thai* was Mike Anderson, who promoted full-contact events from 1974. In these events there is no pretext of Asian philosophy or style. In kickboxing there are no *kata* and all terminology is in English.[28]

Aside from the worldwide influence of *Muay Thai* on various martial arts, Thailand is interesting to the martial artist for other reasons. Thailand has been the sole Southeast Asian country to escape Western colonialism. The chief reason for a strong Indo-Sino influence is that, in defeating and absorbing the Khmer Kingdom into its own culture, Thailand took unto itself all of the very strong Indian and Chinese cultural traits that therein lay.

Additionally, there has been a substantial "overseas" Chinese community of around two million people living in Thailand for centuries. Though most are officially Thai citizens, these Chinese have preserved most of their ethnic practices, including social clubs, secret societies, and *ch'uan fa* associations. The latter are found in most of Thailand's larger cities, and have, for the most part, remained segregated in order to preserve their uniquely Chinese identity. On the other hand, small groups of native Thai through the years have managed to penetrate this world and learn many, if not all, of the secrets of Chinese *ch'uan fa.*

Today, Thai boxing remains the best known Thai art, but *Muay Thai* is all but forgotten in American sports programming; however, its legacy, full-contact and kickboxing contests, is popular in the 1990s.

In California, according to The Muay Thai Academy of America (MTAA) Instructor Surapuk Jamjuntr, there are five or six *Muay Thai* schools in Southern California that are a promotional group providing fighters to all corners of the globe. In the MTAA gym in North Hollywood, adults and children of various nationalities can be seen practicing this old but deadly fighting style.

Indonesia

The important role of geographical location in the development of a country's cultural patterns is particularly in evidence in Indonesia. Situated as it is on the trade route between China on the one hand and India, Western Asia, and Europe on the other, Indonesia has had great exposure to both Asian and European cultures.

The first inhabitants of the Indonesian archipelago are thought to have migrated both from mainland Southeast Asia and from south China about 2000 B.C.[29] These peoples had just completed their stone-age cycle and were entering a bronze-age culture when, in the first century A.D., Hinduism and Buddhism made inroads into their civilization.[30] The strong effects of these two great religious systems are thought to have inspired the rapid rise of such empires as the Srivijaya (SREE-vee-ja-ya) on the island of Sumatra, the Sailendra dynasty of Java, and the Majapahit (MO-jo-paheet) of East Java. Due largely to their borrowings from these well-established mainland cultures, Indonesia's empires flourished, and thus completely dominated the sociological development of all the member islands. Contact with India and China was maintained by each major Indonesian ruler in turn, and so these countries became the two great sources for Indonesia's weaponless martial art development.

There is insufficient historical evidence from which to infer with certainty which of these countries—India or China—gave Indonesia its first exposure to unarmed combat. And the situation is further complicated by the fact that Chinese, Arab, Malay, and Filipino pirates continually disrupted the rather sublime life of the Indonesians both at sea and in their coastal villages. For many of the Indonesian natives, therefore, it was a matter of perfecting an effective fighting technique or being slaughtered.

In modern-day Indonesia four terms—*pukulan, pentjak, silat,* and *kun-tao*—are used to describe unarmed combat in general, much as in the Western world we refer to essentially the same sport by the variant terms "boxing," "pugilism," "fisticuffs," etc. Speaking generally, *pukulan, pentjak, silat,* and *kun-tao* refer to variations of the same Indonesian arts that have developed in different geographical areas of the Indonesian archipelago. But technically, whenever one of the first three of the terms is used, reference is being made to a uniquely Indonesian art and is always written in the Bahasa Indonesian language, whereas the fourth term—*kun-tao* (*k'un t'ou*)—refers to a style or styles of Chinese *ch'uan fa* or kung fu, and is written in romanized Chinese.[31]

There are many, many variations on the general themes of *pukulan, pentjak,* and *silat* in contrast to the relatively few forms of Chinese *kun-tao.* The reason is that the Indonesian styles are localized in distinct areas, many being so specialized that they are considered to be the sole "property" of one village. Thus, while there is a proliferation of highly developed forms found in the islands, few inhabitants of Indonesia are able to avail themselves of instruction in more than one style. That style is generally representative of their home village or city, and as village rivalry is often intense, a master of one form of *pukulan, pentjak,* or *silat* would never teach his village's style to an outsider.

An exception to the above rule was found prior to Indonesia's independence from the Netherlands in 1949. Both native Indonesians and Dutch-Indonesians (or Eurasians as they are often called) who were in an upper-income class were able to avail themselves of the benefits of a Western education and consequently held more profitable and prestigious positions in the Indonesian economy. Such people, therefore, lost their close village ties but could, if they sought out the proper connections, learn various types of self-defense. Thus in more modern times we often find that the better-known masters are Dutch-Indonesian, some of whom even reside in Holland.

Because of the great number of village styles that developed, we will list only the most famous of them. When it is remembered that what is presently termed "Indonesia" encompasses an area only slightly smaller than the area of

Rudy Ter Linden in a posture from the *Tji Kalong* or "Bat style."

the United States and that many of the member islands of the archipelago have had little intercourse with the main islands of Sumatra, Java, Borneo, and Celebes, it is easier to see why such a disparity exists.

Common West Java types of *pukulan* include *Tji Bandar* (pronounced CHI BANDAR), a type of defense used by women and children, characterized by slight body movements and small steps of the feet, due largely to the tight-fitting Indonesian *sarong; Tji Monjet* (CHI MOAN-yet) or "ape style"; *Tji Kalong* (CHI KAH-long) or "bat style"; *Tji Matjan* (CHI MAHTjan) or "tiger style"; *Tji Mandih* (CHI MAHN-di), characterized by fluid, sweeping body movements; *Tji Oelar* (CHI OWE-lahr) or "snake style"; and *Serak* (SEAR-awk), which invites attack by allowing an opponent to move close, then defeats him with superior speed and counterpunching.[32]

In East Java the art is generally termed "pentjak." Here also is found a rather heavy settlement of permanent Chinese residents, such that *kun-tao is* another prominent East Javan form. The most significant *kun-tao* styles are: *Minangkabau* (MEE-nang-kah-BAU) of Sumatra; *Khilap* and *Sjatung* (KEY-lahp and SHAN-tung) of Jakarta, capital city of Indonesia; *Soetji Hati* (SUIT-jee HOT-ee) of Central Java; and *Kontak* (KOHN-tahk) found primarily in West Java, which emphasizes punching of nerve centers.[33]

As previously observed, village rivalry is an integral part of Indonesia's culture. The most colorful way in which this is evidenced is in the pitting of the various village champions against one another during festivals held throughout the year. In each village a fighting champion is recognized who, because of his status as a fighting man, is called upon to represent his village's fighting style in combat. At the same time that he presents himself to defend his village honor, young men of his own village may challenge him if they feel they can defeat him. Thus if any of his fellow villagers defeat him, he steps down and a new champion is popularly heralded.

During the numerous holidays that the Indonesians celebrate, the high point of the festivities comes at the end of the day when a circular ring is formed outdoors for challenges to be met. Depending on the importance of the village holding such tourneys, fighting masters come out for these displays who are not normally seen at all during the balance of the year, and so it is exciting to everyone involved. Since training in his village's particular form of combat is a part of every young boy's education, there is not one of them who is not eager to see his village's chief protagonist pit his art against the others.

Actual combat takes place in the evening, the highlight of a long day of festive merriment. Torches are secured to long poles and planted in the ground in a circular pattern. As darkness approaches and the torches are lit, villagers anticipating the evening's entertainment begin congregating on the periphery of the illuminated circle, each hopeful that their local champion will emerge victorious.

Fighters from other localities move into the front rows and wait to see the popular favorite. Drummers kneel to one side of the "arena," poised for the drama. With the entire village thus situated, the village champion and a female partner carrying a silken scarf enter the circle of light and begin the well-known *kambangan* (kahm-BAHNG-an) or flower dance. This is an uncannily graceful series of movements that demands the utmost physical conditioning in order to be properly executed. The throbbing drums bring the dance to its conclusion and the woman melts away into the crowd, leaving her scarf in the center of the ring.

This act of dropping the scarf signals the beginning of a fighting dance and also acts as the invitation for the fighters in the audience to try their combat skills with the figure in the circle. As the drumming tempo increases, the master performs the formal and stylized *langkas* and *djuroes* (JEW-rows), dancelike fighting movements that appear similar to the various karate *kata,* but that lack the stiff formality thereof. If the man's performance is flawless, the evening's entertainment might end at that point with no challengers risking defeat. If, on the other hand, the local master showed a weakness in his movements, a challenger invariably springs from the crowd and the battle begins in earnest. Interestingly enough, a footsweep causing an opponent to fall is oftentimes the margin of victory. If, however, the person knocked to the ground refuses to concede victory, a bloody contest will ensue in which death is not uncommon for one of the combatants. The footsweeping technique is still generally the basis for victory in these formal competitions, and as odd as this may seem on first thought, it becomes obvious that this is supremely logical, since at the level of adroitness that these men find themselves, where a hundredth of a second of timing becomes all-important, any man who is sufficiently superior to his opponent to upset him with a footsweep will invariably be superior in actual combat.

Malaysia

The Malay Peninsula extends down through the heart of Southeast Asia, acting as a bridge to Indonesia and the islands of the western Pacific. Malaysian peoples share with other Southeast Asians a widespread religious and cultural heritage from India. It is also very likely that India influenced the development of a weaponless system of fighting called *bersilat* (bur-SEE-lot); however, there is more direct evidence at the present time to support the common hypothesis that China was the real spiritual force behind *bersilat's* evolution in Malaysia.

Bersilat in translation means "self-defense," but according to a popular legend its origin is said to have been traced to a woman named "Bersilat" who, through a series of dreams, acquired a knowledge of the fundamentals of empty-handed fighting.[34] Other than this legend, there are very few written materials to be found giving the history of the art.

Malaysian weddings and other festive occasions are almost always highlighted by *bersilat* exhibitions, and in some instances actual fighting contests can even be seen as part of the entertainment.[35] *Bersilat* exists today in two forms: One, *Silat Pulat,* is purely for public display and exhibition, while the other form, called *Silat Buah,* is used in actual combat.[36]

Exhibition *bersilat* is probably the more graceful of the two forms. It is greatly stylized and artificial in its execution, having as its base a system of conventional gestures and movements that are entirely prearranged. Again, like its Indonesian counterparts (i.e., *pukulan, pentjak, silat,* and *kun-tao),* musical and rhythmic accompaniment are used for *bersilat* in exhibition.

The deadly *Silat Buah is* generally practiced in semiseclusion. Here, the secret moves are passed on from master to disciple under a vow of secrecy,[37] reminiscent of Chinese *ch'uan fa.* Various forms of *Silat Buah* can be found throughout the narrow peninsula of Malaysia, but the most popular forms are fist and finger striking, grappling and using locks, throws, and various grips, and a spectacular style that utilizes high leaps and flying kicks.

Bersilat varies from state to state in Malaysia, and indeed from teacher to teacher, but the east coast of Malaysia is generally considered to have the best men of the art. *Kun-tao is* also practiced in the larger cities where numerous Chinese clubs exist, and where a rivalry between *kun-tao* associations and *bersilat* groups exists. Little information is known about the resulting clashes that occur between these rival factions.

With the the use of the *kris* as the basic means for fighting, the passing of the war years—both world and civil—and with a more readily disciplined and law-abiding citizenry, *bersilat* as a secret art of combat is slowly giving way to *bersilat* as a sport and means of physical exercise.[38]

A tape-recorded interview at the University of Malaysia with *bersilat* expert Abdul Samat, was conducted by Dr. B. C. Stone and Dr. G. B. Evans:

DR. STONE: What does *bersilat* mean in English?

MR. SAMAT: In English, *bersilat* means "self-defense." The name "bersilat" itself comes from a woman's name—"Bersilat." She is said to have learned the various forms of unarmed combat in her sleep.

DR. STONE: In other words she learned the techniques of self-defense in a dream?

MR. SAMAT: Yes.

DR. STONE: Did *bersilat* originate in Malaysia?

MR. SAMAT: No, it originated in Sumatra.

DR. STONE: How long ago was this?

MR. SAMAT: In 1511.

DR. STONE: Did the Malaysians or the Sumatrans have a soldier or military class such as the Indian *Kshatriya* or the Japanese samurai? If so, did they practice *bersilat?*

MR. SAMAT: In Sumatra, I do not know, but here they have a military caste that is trained in *bersilat.*

DR. STONE: What do they call these soldiers?

MR. SAMAT: *Ten-tera* or Royal Army.

DR. STONE: Would these soldiers be attached to the court of a sultan?

MR. SAMAT: Yes. Each tribe and each village in Malaysia has leaders who group their men into local armies. When the sultan of a district needs men to fight a war, he tells his village leaders to call upon their men.

DR. STONE: Has there been any Chinese influence in *bersilat?*

MR. SAMAT: Lately there has been Chinese influence.

DR. STONE: You mean that Chinese influence on the development of *bersilat is* a modern development?

MR. SAMAT: Yes, especially the Peking style of *kun-tao.* We have not had Peking style before. Prior to this influence, kicking with the leg was considered very rude. This would be for exhibition style only, of course; in real self-defense any part of the body could be used.

DR. STONE: Then the Chinese influence would be found only in the real fighting and not in the exhibition category of *bersilat?*

MR. SAMAT: Yes.

DR. STONE: Would you say the exhibition form of *bersilat* is the closest thing to the old forms of *bersilat?*

MR. SAMAT: Yes, this form follows the old culture.

DR. STONE: In karate and kung fu, there are certain movement exercises. In *bersilat,* do students learn such movements utilizing the attacking aspects of the art? In other words, do students learn certain dancelike movements and definite sequences having a specific name?

MR. SAMAT: No, each movement does not have a distinct name, but the student has to learn the movements step-by-step. The first movement in *bersilat* is to learn the breakfall and then the student goes on learning each movement up to a total of forty-four.

DR. STONE: If you were actually in a fight, would you change the sequence of these steps?

MR. SAMAT: In a real fight you would normally use whatever movements are the most convenient to you.

DR. STONE: Then one would have to have a complete memory of all the steps and be able to pick out instantly the one form or forms you would use?

MR. SAMAT: Yes. You must always have an eye on the enemy, and especially the head and shoulders.

DR. STONE: Why is this?

MR. SAMAT: Because if the enemy wants to kick you, his head moves. If he wants to spear you with a weapon or punch you, the shoulders move. These are the keys.

DR. STONE: What parts of the body are used as weapons in *bersilat?*

MR. SAMAT: The heel of the palm, the little finger and the

side of the palm, the elbow, the shoulder, the knee, the balls of the feet, the heel of the foot, and your head, too.

DR. STONE: Do you have ways of training these various parts of the body making them tougher?

MR. SAMAT: Oh yes!

DR. STONE: How do you train, by punching things?

MR. SAMAT: The usual thing is to put sand into a sack of some sort and punch this every day. Later on, punching trees of a certain variety hardens the knuckles. This takes at least forty-four days and one cannot stop it even for a single day, or if one's hand bleeds from the pounding.

DR. STONE: Would a *bersilat* student usually choose a tree that had a smooth bark?

MR. SAMAT: Usually, any convenient tree is chosen.

DR. EVANS: What type of tree do you use?

MR. SAMAT: I use the Jack Fruit tree, and, normally, you are expected to practice this punching until the tree dies.

DR. STONE: Do you have stunts or demonstrations, such as breaking pieces of wood or bricks, or something of that nature?

MR. SAMAT: We do not have this practice in *bersilat,* but we could break these things.

DR. EVANS: Do you ever practice striking bamboo?

MR. SAMAT: No, this is too dangerous because bamboo cuts you very easily.

DR. STONE: Moving on to another area. Are there national or local competitions in *bersilat?* Would you have a national or local champion?

MR. SAMAT: Yes, they have such things nowadays.

DR. STONE: Is there one for each state?

MR. SAMAT: Contests are held at local festivals and celebrations.

DR. STONE: How often do they hold these competitions?

MR. SAMAT: Usually, once a year.

DR. EVANS: Is it stopped now? I understood they stopped having the contests since last year (1965).

DR. STONE: Why is that?

MR. SAMAT: I really do not know, but maybe the funds for these competitions are gone.

DR. STONE: Does this mean that fewer people are studying *bersilat* now?

MR. SAMAT: Actually more people studying *bersilat* now.

DR. STONE: But they have ended the championships now?

MR. SAMAT: Yes.

DR. STONE: What does the government think about *bersilat?* Is it government supported?

MR. SAMAT: There seems to be no official government position concerning the art.

DR. STONE: Do you know of any influence from other Southeast Asian countries?

MR. SAMAT: I do not know.

DR. EVANS: When you were trained, were there other students present?

MR. SAMAT: There were three of us.

DR. EVANS: Did you practice the movement steps together?

MR. SAMAT: No, some students take longer to pass each step.

DR. STONE: Describe the colors of the costume you wear in *bersilat.*

MR. SAMAT: In the beginning the costume is white, and the second step the dress is black. The third step has a black, white, and red costume. That is, white trousers and shirt, black sash, and a red jacket. An instructor wears all green.

DR. EVANS: What about the headdress?

MR. SAMAT: The headdress is normally red for all those who complete the final step. When you become an assistant instructor you wear a green one.

DR. EVANS: Have you done any instructing?

MR. SAMAT: Yes I have.

DR. STONE: Have you studied other styles of *bersilat?*

MR. SAMAT: Not styles, but types. One from Java, and the *Minangkabau* form from Sumatra.

DR. STONE: How do these types differ from *bersilat?*

MR. SAMAT: They have different steps and movements.

DR. STONE: Is one supposed to be better than another?

MR. SAMAT: Well, I find the *Sjatung* form quite good. Better even than the *Minangkabau* and other Javanese forms.

DR. STONE: How many types or styles are there?

MR. SAMAT: We have in Malaysia the Javanese *silat,* the Sumatran *Minangkabau,* the *Bayan silat,* the *Sjatung silat,* and the *Kontak silat.* This last form is very dangerous because it attacks the nerve centers.

DR. EVANS: You mean they strike the sensitive areas of the body?

MR. SAMAT: Yes, they usually chop these places.

DR. EVANS: In *bersilat,* I believe they use no weapons. Is this correct?

MR. SAMAT: No, in *bersilat* they use a short stick, club, or actually anything. In Malaysia the *kris* (knife) is often used. The use of certain knives is an Islamic influence. There is also some Arabic influence in some of the steps.

DR. EVANS: When you strike do you make a noise?

MR. SAMAT: Yes, to frighten the enemy.

DR. EVANS: Do you learn distraction methods to fool your opponent?

MR. SAMAT: Yes, this is done. There are many of these techniques.

DR. EVANS: Did you learn any of these feinting methods?

MR. SAMAT: These are learned only by attackers, so I did not learn them.

DR. EVANS: When you are using *bersilat* in combat do you watch an opponent's eyes as well as his head and shoulders?

MR. SAMAT: Yes, all parts of the head.

DR. STONE: Do you watch his legs as well?

MR. SAMAT: No. When the leg moves the head will also move. If the head does not move, the strike will lack power and not hurt you.

DR. STONE: Has the training of *bersilat* ever been written down?

MR. SAMAT: As far as I know it has not been written down.

DR. STONE: Then you would say one learns this art by personal communication with the instructor?

MR. SAMAT: Yes. It is very difficult to describe each step.

DR. EVANS: What did you find to be the hardest thing to learn in your *bersilat* training?

MR. SAMAT: The breakfall is the hardest.

Bersilat today remains one of the world's rarest fighting arts due to the intense secrecy with which it evolved in Malaysia. So little has been written about the art that few *ch'uan fa* and karate experts know anything of *bersilat* or Malaysian fighting arts in general. Those persons interested in this esoteric Southeast Asian martial art can find more information in articles published in the *Journal of the Straits Malayan Branch Royal Asiatic Society* over the last fifty years. Exact data can be found in the "Bibliography of Malaya," edited in two volumes by Cheeseman and Beda Lim, *JSMBRAS* of 1960 and 1961.[39]

Philippines

That the Philippine archipelago developed martial arts similar to those of East Asia is not surprising, especially in light of the fact that these seven thousand plus islands lie in the trading paths for the China and Southeast Asia trade. Consequently, it is possible to see that diverse martial art forms developed there that were not all interrelated. Eclecticism is the hallmark of the fighting systems in the Philippines. In observing Chinese kung fu or Japanese karate, or many of the Indonesian forms of *bersilat*, most uninitiated would see little difference in their styles or forms within that system. This would never be the case in the Philippines. To the same uninitiated observer, styles from different regions would look completely different from one another.[40] Adding to this diversity, and confusing somewhat the study of Filipino fighting arts, is the numerous languages and dialects whereby similar forms might have different names depending on the region of the country.

Of all the martial arts examined in this study, only the Filipino form of stick fighting can boast of having its practitioners dispatch a famous world figure—Ferdinand Magellan. This happened in 1521 when the navigator and sea captain was killed by Filipinos wielding rattan and hardwood sticks.[41]

Ferdinand Magellan was a Portuguese nobleman in the employ of the Spanish King Charles I. He won approval in 1519 to forge a passage around the tip of South America and establish a route to the East Indies.[42] After an arduous and erratic voyage, Magellan arrived in the Philippines in 1521. The Captain was excited to see natives wearing gold ornaments and he thought he must be near China. On April 27, 1521, Magellan landed on Cebu Island and for reasons not completely clear became immediately embroiled in local politics. He made a treaty with a local chieftain and joined with him in an armed foray against another chief named Lapu Lapu.[43] In the skirmish that ensued on Mactan Island, Magellan was killed, some claim by Chief Lapu Lapu himself.[44]

Magellan's crew, in part, escaped and went on to complete the first circumnavigation of the globe. Magellan is forever linked with this navigational feat; however, his mortal remains stayed behind on Mactan Island as a trophy of war.

Magellan's death did not end Spanish attempts to conquer the Philippines. In a 333-year struggle, Spain would eventually triumph, at least territorially.

In the years before the Spanish, Filipinos had learned many ways of fighting from invaders, and native forms were improved to combat foreign onslaught.[45] To see this in its proper context, one must look at the theories concerning human habitation of this archipelago.

Anthropologists today still debate the sources of human migration to the Philippines. One theory claims that Egyptians in reed boats first arrived in the archipelago in Ancient times. Still other social scientists have judged the first inhabitants to be émigrés from India and Iran.[46]

Most Anthropologists today agree that Negrito pygmy peoples were in the Philippines before any other invaders arrived in force. The Negrito were later pushed into the mountainous interior by conquering Indonesians in the northern islands and by Malays in the southern area, perhaps as early as 300 B.C. Modern Filipinos are a mixture of these two groups, plus Spanish, Chinese, and American heritage as well. The Negritos were expert with the bow and arrow, whereas the Indonesians and Malays favored bladed weapons.[47]

In the ninth century A.D., T'ang Chinese established relations with the Philippines and introduced their various forms of *ch'uan fa*. Chinese colonies emerged in these islands during this dynastic period and exist in large numbers even now.

Islam began its spread in the Southern Philippines in the fifteenth century, culminating in the Malaccan Empire.[48]

When the Spanish arrived in force in the sixteenth and seventeenth centuries, eclectic fighting forms were the norm.

There are over one hundred styles of Filipino martial arts today, but they are usually divided into three major groups. There are the Northern, Central, and Southern styles. These forms utilize an array of weapons and sundry uses of commonplace items such as newspapers, chairs, fans, etc.[49] The common denominator of many of the Filipino styles is the principle that combat is based on a pattern of angles of attack.[50] The same basic defenses for each angle are effective no matter what weapons or techniques are used. When these angles are mastered, the bare hands and countless weapons become the arsenal for effective fighting. This is a relatively modern development in the Filipino martial arts.

Kali is considered the oldest form of fighting in the Philippines and utilizes sticks, blades, and empty-hand combat.[51] *Kalis* are Malay swords that were brought to the Philippines.[52] With the arrival of the Spanish, *kali* went underground and devotees can be seen following much the same clandestine history of other martial arts forced underground by a foreign threat.

Kali was the precursor to other Filipino styles that developed from this ancient art. Some of the major ones are:

LANGUAGE	SYSTEM
Ibanog	Pangkalikali
Tagalog	Pananondata
Visayan	Kiliradman
Ilongo	Pagaradman
Ilocano	Kabaroan
Pampangueno	Siniwali
Pangasinese	Kalirongan[53]

In *kali* there are twelve basic weapon forms. According to *kali* instructor Tim Tackett these forms include:

1. single stick or sword
2. double stick or swords
3. stick and dagger
4. single dagger
5. double dagger
6. spear, staff, and oar
7. empty hands (which includes punching, kicking, wrestling, locking, and knee and elbow arts)
8. flexible weapons like whips, etc.
9. projectile weapons such as blowguns
10. pocket stick, like *yawara*
11. *dos manos,* like Japanese kendo
12. thrusting weapons

There is also another form of empty-handed fighting of Chinese origin called *kun-tao,* practiced mostly in Sulu.[54] *Kun-tao* is a term from the Fukienese Chinese dialect used to describe the arts of that province in China. *Kempo, kun-tao,* and *ch'uan fa* are different readings of the same Chinese characers. Because of its Chinese descent and name, few sources concerning native Filipino forms ever mention this art.

With Spanish rule intact about 1600, and weaponry outlawed in general, Filipino martial arts were being practiced clandestinely, similar to karate in the Ryukyu Islands, curiously about the same time, in the early seventeenth and eighteenth centuries. Out of this period of Spanish conquest came the term *eskrima* (or *escrima*). Some believe the term originated from the stick-fighting forms that gave Magellan and other Conquistadors much grief and pain and is from the Spanish word "escaramuza" meaning "skirmish." At any rate, the term "eskrima" has become popular, like kung fu, to describe forms of fighting.

There is another term used to describe a system of Filipino fighting: *arnis de mano,* or simply *arnis.* This is derived from the Spanish word *arnes,* meaning "trappings" or "defensive armor."[55] This form is sometimes considered a different style of Filipino fighting; however, it is actually another term for *eskrima.*[56] The Visayans used the term "eskrima" instead of "arnis," and the two terms have coexisted through the years much like kung fu and *ch'uan fa* have in the Chinese martial arts. *Eskrima* and *arnis* are essentially the same thing, though followers of the two forms might argue otherwise.

One of the notable features in *arnis* combat is the continuous striking patterns in a figure-eight form; even if hits are scored, the attack completes the figure-eight pattern.[57] The figure-eight pattern can be vertical, horizontal, or any path in between. The weapons used can be knives, sticks, or bare hands.

Historically, *arnis* and *eskrima* incorporated three related methods: *espada y daga* (sword and dagger), using a short knife and a long blade; *solo baston* (single stick); and *sinawali* (to weave, which utilizes two equal length sticks that are "twirled" in a weaving motion for blocking and striking).[58]

With all of the chaos associated with years of Marcos rule in the Philippines, it is not surprising that thousands of Filipinos have left their islands to start a new life abroad. The United States has been their primary destination. When one investigates the early years of American-Filipino relations, it becomes clear why many Filipinos preferred to practice their martial arts privately. The historical picture of the U.S. in the Philippines is not pretty and has some very similar nuances to America's later struggle in Vietnam.

America's imperialistic hopes of continued expansion after the subjugation of the American Indian led to visions

Mark Wiley demonstrates the use of the *eskrima* stick and dagger.

of Pacific Rim conquests. Hawaii was annexed in 1898 (see Chap. 9, p. 134), and this year was to prove pivotal in further excursions in the Pacific. These ideas of expanding an American "empire" were brought on by big business interests, jingoists, "yellow journalism," and big navy enthusiasts, to name some of the reasons. This prompted America's first Asian war in 1898, the Spanish-American War.

At first the Filipinos hailed the U.S. victory because they envisioned independence from Spain. What they found instead was simply another colonial master, the United States. U.S. President William McKinley was quoted after the war's end saying that he simply could not let the Philippines go alone, "that there was nothing left for us to do but take them all and to educate the Filipinos, and uplift and civilize and Christianize them . . . ."[59] Emilio Aguinaldo, a

Filipino leader who helped American forces against the Spanish, then decided to fight the newest foreign invaders and became leader of the *insurrectos* to fight the United States. He had dreamed of independence, but America quickly wanted these islands for business reasons. War broke out between the *insurrectos* and the United States in 1899.

American historians have a way of softening events like those that occurred in the Filipino-American War of 1899–1902. Until very recently this event has been portrayed in U.S. history texts as a mild guerrilla subduing campaign. It was in fact pre-Vietnam "search and destroy," with all of the sinister consequences implied.

In January 1900, Senator Albert Beveridge spoke for the majority economic and political interests of the country, "It has been charged that our conduct of the war has been cruel. Senators, it has been the reverse . . . We must remember that we are not dealing with Americans or Europeans. We are dealing with Orientals."[60]

In the jungles of the Philippines, American servicemen met with insects, dangerous animals, disease, and rattan and knife-wielding Filipinos intent on protecting their homeland. Combat was fierce, with atrocities committed by both sides. Racism was rampant in the United States at this time and these feelings were carried to the Philippine War where American "boys" were fighting "colored" Filipinos. To illustrate, a Marine Major named Waller asked instructions of a General Smith and was told, "that it was no time to take prisoners, and that he was to make Samar a howling wilderness. Major Waller asked General Smith to define the age limit for killing, and he replied 'everything over ten.'"[61] In Batangas Province it was estimated that one-third of the population of 300,000 were killed by combat, famine, and disease directly related to the war.[62]

One may question whether this type of historical reporting is germane to a martial arts work; however, it becomes abundantly clear when we understand that racism played a role in why the martial arts practiced by Chinese, Japanese, Okinawans, Koreans, and Filipinos were done so in guarded secrecy, at least initially. Even in the countries of origin these same martial arts were secretive.

In the United States, many immigrant Filipinos heard bloody tales from their fathers and grandfathers about the brutality of the United States during the war of independence against American imperialism. Is it any wonder then that until the 1960s *eskrima* was taught to the Filipino community alone?

In the 1920s, *arnis* gained popularity in the Philippines. Masters were called "eskrimadors,"[63] again showing the linkage between *arnis* and *eskrima.* After World War II, *arnis* changed. The influence of judo, karate, and aikido led to modifications in the mainstream Filipino martial arts, and some older styles were abandoned.

In 1951, Ciriaco C. Canete (a modern Filipino master) developed *Eskrido,* blending elements of *eskrima,* judo, and aikido.[64] There followed a wave of martial arts enthusiasm in the Philippines.

In the 1970s, a popular Filipino television program featured karate versus *arnis* contests where the combatants wore protective gear.[65] Depending on the area of the Philippines, terminology is overly abundant. The arts of *arnis de mano* were mistakenly thought by many Filipinos to be of Spanish origin. Consequently, for a time, those methods considered native to the islands gained favor. However, *arnis* and *eskrima,* as systems of forms, strikes, etc. are now the most popular terms for the Filipino martial arts.

In the early 1970s Professor Remy Presas introduced the Modern Arnis system in the United States. His style of *arnis,* which is popular in Negros Occidental and Manila, is one of the most popular of the Filipino martial arts in North America and Europe.

In the 1970s President Ferdinand Marcos, in context with his National Fitness Program, saw that *arnis* was incorporated in the high school physical education program.[66] Now *arnis* is the national sport of the Philippines.

Other styles currently popular in the Philippines include *Doce Pares eskrima, Kali Ilustrisimo, Sikiran, Pekiti Tirsia,* and *Lapu Lapu kali.*

琉球

CHAPTER 5
OKINAWA

OKINAWA was generally absent from the mainstream of world history until 1945 when it served as the scene for the epic showdown battle between the two military giants of the Pacific Ocean, Japan and the American Allied forces. This sequestered island, however, has been the site of many an intrigue between Japan and China, and has itself, at one time or another, been embroiled in life-and-death power struggles with both of these great Asian political rivals.

Okinawa, the principal island of the Ryukyu archipelago, literally means "a rope in the offing."[1] An apt description indeed, as this long slender island lies near the center of a line of islands that stretch from Japan in the north to the very doorstep of China in the south. The prevailing winds and the Japan

Current sweep away from continental Asia close to the Ryukyus, and on past Japan into the North Pacific. Okinawa was truly a "rope in the offing" for those unfortunate mainland sailors who found themselves forced out into the open sea with no apparent rescue at hand. We shall see these shipwrecked castaways to be an integral part of our story.

The southernmost island of the Ryukyu chain is visible from the island of Taiwan. The northernmost island over seven hundred miles away lies within miles of Kyushu, the southernmost of Japan's four major islands.[2] Between these extremities are 140 islands, only thirty-six of which are permanently settled.[3]

The origin of the Okinawan people is one of those fascinating anthropological mysteries. There are strong indications that Okinawa's first inhabitants were the survivors of an ancient shipwreck, the chance result of one of the vicious typhoons for which the area is noted. If such is the case, historians will forever be deprived of the valuable written materials usually found in connection with the volitional movement and migration of peoples. If, on the other hand, man reached the Ryukyus in Paleolithic or Neolithic times, as some evidence suggests, written materials would again be virtually nonexistent.

Besides our hypothetical castaways, who depended for survival upon what they could forage from the countryside, there were occasional immigrations of peoples from the north who brought with them household belongings, domestic animals, tools, and religious items. It appears that these immigrations were quite infrequent, and that there have been no new immigrations into Okinawa of any consequence within the last two thousand years.[4] Thus the general patterns of Ryukyuan culture were established over two millennia ago.

The physiognomy of the Okinawans more closely resembles the Japanese than any other Asian people. However, many Okinawans are found with Southeast Asian physical characteristics, thus indicating a strong strain of Malayo-Polynesian blood. There is a very positive Southeast Asian influence on the architecture of the Ryukyuan chain, and there are a number of linguistic similarities, although the language forms throughout the Ryukyus have a much stronger affinity with archaic Japanese. We know that there were Ryukyuan contacts with the Asian continent as early as the third century B.C., a fact that is shown by the number of artifacts identified with north China that have been found near Naha, the present capital of Okinawa.[5] The inevitable conclusion, then, is that there were cultural influences that found their way into the Ryukyu Islands from the east, from the north, and from the south,[6] and that Okinawan culture is a blending of these elements.

For our purposes, the significance of these findings lies only in the fact that sometime, from one or more of these three outside areas, there came an influx of weaponless fighting techniques that were the progenitors of modern-day karate. As we saw earlier, China saw the development of the Shaolin *ch'uan fa* by the Indian monk Bodhidharma in the sixth century, and, though there may have been some kind of weaponless fighting as early as the third century B.C., it did not develop into an organized system of unarmed self-defense until after Bodhidharma's advent.

China's Influence on Okinawan Karate

China's earliest planned contact with the Ryukyus came during the Sui dynasty (A.D. 581–618). This period was one of intellectual intrigue instigated by Emperor Yang Chien's attempts to find the secrets of eternal life and a means of turning base metals into gold.[7] Yang Chien outfitted a number of expeditions to "barbarian" lands in his search for the legendary "Land of Happy Immortals" to the east.[8] During one of these forays in the seventh century (*ca.* A.D. 608) a number of islands were found in the eastern seas. But the inhabitants were far from being "Happy Immortals." This we know from later reports by the expedition's commander, in which it was related that many of the inhabitants of one specific island lost their lives during a skirmish with Chinese marines of the expeditionary force. Although the exact location of the islands that were the subject of this report was never factually determined, various authorities have taken the stand that they were in the Ryukyu group, and that the besieged island was probably Okinawa. This deduction is based in large part upon the fact that soon after Emperor Yang Chien's rule, Chinese documents began referring to all of the islands between Japan and the Philippines as "Liu Ch'iu," using the ideographs that are pronounced in Japanese as "Ryukyu" (rhee-you-cue).[9]

By the seventh century, China had officially recognized Japan as an independent political entity. At various times official diplomatic and cultural missions comprised of Japanese priests, soldiers, and statesmen passed between the Chinese mainland and Japan. A few of these missions were reported missing, with no explanation as to why. We can only surmise that the immediate cause for such disappearances was shipwreck, and that the survivors became inhabitants of islands out of the mainstream of diplomatic travel. What specific influence these survivors had on the development of primitive Ryukyuan culture is not precisely known, but educated speculation leads us to believe that it was far reaching.

Did these travelers bring a karate-like art to Okinawa? This theory is plausible, as members of the Japanese warrior class or samurai generally escorted these missions. Also, peripatetic Buddhist priests and scholars commuted regularly between Japan and China in the seventh and eighth centuries, and we have seen (in Chap. 2) that such individuals were often deft proponents of unarmed self-defense techniques. Japanese students of Buddhism studying in Chinese monasteries were undoubtedly exposed to the Shaolin techniques of the monk Bodhidharma, and it is reported that many of the more adventurous of these, after completing their training, set sail eastward in order to spread the teachings to the known world. Such monks, if stranded on a distant island in the Ryukyus, would doubtlessly have introduced the natives to their form of self-defense as well as to their religion. But again, there is no concrete proof of such occurrences, and so such possibilities must remain in the realm of conjecture.

There is a widely held hypothesis that *ch'uan fa* entered the Ryukyus via China's Foochow district during the sixth- and seventh-century reign of China's Sui dynasty.[10] Such Chinese-Ryukyuan contacts are first mentioned in the section on "Eastern Barbarians" of the *Sui Shu,* the dynastic history of the Sui rulers.[11] Then again, the definitive Japanese encyclopedia, *Sekai Dai-Hyakkajiten,* states that karate or a type of *ch'uan fa* was probably brought to Okinawa from China during the T'ang dynasty (A.D. 618–907).[12]

Possibly the strongest support for the claim that karate is an innate part of Okinawan culture is based on some of the Ryukyu islanders' classical dances. The parts danced by males during certain festivals resemble modern karate movements. Add to this the fact that these festivals have been performed since earliest recorded history, and there seems to be a fair case for Okinawan dancing being a precursor to karate.[13] But, as we cannot tell where these dances came from, it may be concluded that Chinese influence on Okinawan weaponless combat did not occur until later in the fourteenth century. From the end of the T'ang dynasty to the beginning of the Ming dynasty in 1368—a span of

450 years—there is an unexplained silence regarding the development of karate in the Ryukyus. Not only is there a dearth of written materials on the subject, but even oral traditions concerning the art are vague and generally lacking. Certainly, had *ch'uan fa* been introduced to Okinawa between the Sui and Ming dynasties and found acceptance in the Ryukyuan culture, evidence of it would be readily locatable in Ryukyuan cultural annals.

In 1372 official Chinese-Okinawan relations were instituted when Okinawa's King Satto expressed his allegiance to the Ming emperor of China. In so doing, the Okinawan king not only relegated his domain to tributary status, but also threw open Okinawa's watery doors to greatly intensified Chinese cultural influence.[14] With Okinawa now a Chinese satellite, cultural proselytization began in earnest. In the following centuries *ch'uan fa* found its way into the Ryukyus thus aiding the establishment of a regular system of unarmed self-defense, based partly on the indigenous Okinawan form of fighting with fists.

This ancient Okinawan style of combat was termed *tode* (toe-day). Many Japanese historians and Okinawan karate masters feel that in spite of the lack of supportive evidence, this art is native to the Ryukyu Islands, and that when *tode* was combined with other fighting styles introduced from Asia, the art of karate evolved. Therefore, among the Orientalists who have studied Okinawan military history and martial art development, there is a general agreement that *ch'uan fa* is only partly responsible for the birth of present-day Okinawan karate. (The author concurs with this assumption only to the point that the closed-fist technique of modern karate, because of its long use in the Ryukyus as a primary means of wartime survival and its resulting emphasis on maiming and killing, is "native" to the Ryukyus, though he feels that it had its ultimate beginning in the Chinese art of *ch'uan fa*.)

The oral transmission of historical events is often more reliable than written records. In Okinawa, since little recorded data has been found on the history of karate, we look to the oral traditions that cite the beginning of the fourteenth century as the period when a karate-like art began to be practiced generally. This art was greatly stimulated by the mission of Chinese officials and their entourage, sent to Okinawa by Emperor Hung Wu in 1372. Needless to say, the exponents of *ch'uan fa* in this group made a positive impression on interested Okinawans.

During the Ming dynasty (1368–1644) a permanent Okinawan settlement began to develop on Chinese soil at the Chinese capital of Ch'uan-chou. In terms of lasting Chinese influence upon Okinawan history, this settlement was extremely important; for not only did commuting Okinawan citizens bring back to their islands artifacts and customs, but they brought a general belief that all things Chinese were indeed superior.[15] Although in a historical sense Chinese influence was slow in reaching the more remote areas of the Ryukyus, it did, in time, penetrate to even the most isolated islands so that the blending of cultures was eventually complete. These firm cultural ties were to last for five hundred years.[16]

The year 1393 saw a sudden spurt in the migration of Chinese people to Okinawa. This was the result of an imperial gift from China in the form of a large body of skilled artisans and merchants.[17] This group of Chinese, which soon had formed into its own community, has long been referred to as the "Thirty-six Families." Such numeration of people with a homogeneity of purpose has been common in Chinese society. Yet in this case the term refers to a much larger number; i.e., to Okinawa's Chinese community as a whole. Oral tradition states that these "Thirty-six Families" were largely responsible for the spread of *ch'uan fa* throughout the Ryukyu Islands.[18]

Unification and International Trade

In 1429 Okinawa became a unified kingdom under the dynamic leadership of a man named Hashi. Hashi, following the ages-old Chinese and Japanese practice of "rule from the wings," appointed his father King of Chuzan, since Chuzan was at that time the most important of the three Okinawan principalities of Chuzan, Hokuzan, and Nanzan.[19] Shortly after acquiring control of the land, Hashi renamed these principalities, changing Chuzan to Nakagami, Hokuzan to Kunigami, and Nanzan to Shimajiri.[20]

Okinawa at first profited little from this unification, as the peasants and quasi-nobility, called *anji,* still lived for the most part at the same bare subsistence level as that of their ancestors. But this was soon to change. Because of his exposure to Chinese government officials and a knowledge of Okinawa's isolated position, Hashi learned a great deal about improving economic conditions in his country. One of his first lessons involved the great importance of active trade relations with other countries. Since Ryukyuans had long been able seafarers, they quite naturally fell into their newly appointed roles as commercial sea traders.[21] Thus for the following two centuries Okinawa's two large towns, Shuri and Naha, became famous as centers of an increasingly profitable traffic in luxury goods, since wares purchased in the Indies and the bazaars of Southeast Asia were brought to Okinawa and reshipped to China, Korea, and Japan.[22]

The effect of this extensive trade on the development of karate is readily apparent when it is realized that Okinawans were suddenly, as it were, having widespread contact with those Arabs, Malays, Indonesians, and Thai who frequented the centers of commerce. Of course, such contact in itself is not enough to assure us of an exchange of ideas on weaponless fighting systems. But when we add two ingredients, bored and lonely seamen, and free-flowing spirits, we suddenly have a stage set for a great deal of volatile cultural interaction. In Chapter 4 we already established the fact that karate-like arts were well developed in Indonesia, Malaysia, Thailand, and other seaport islands in the South China Sea. We therefore arrive at a picture of brawling sailors performing a very picturesque, although undoubtedly bloody, exchange of "ideas" on weaponless fighting techniques. It is a virtual certainty that at this time Okinawans gained most, if not all, of their insight into the Southeast Asian forms of unarmed combat, which is stated unequivocally by the acknowledged authority on Okinawan history, George H. Kerr.[23]

Records in Okinawa's national archives that were, unfortunately, destroyed during World War II, indicated that between 1432 and 1570 Okinawa established forty-four official embassies in Annam (Vietnam), Thailand, Malaysia, and many of the lesser kingdoms of Java.[24] This intercourse is particularly meaningful to us, since it helps to verify a long-held conviction that modern karate kicking techniques were imported from Cambodia and Laos,[25] whereas the open-handed and finger-thrusting techniques evolved from different locations.

Development After the Satsuma Invasion

Probably the single most important date in Okinawan history is 1609. The great Satsuma clan in southern Kyushu (Japan), led by the Shimazu family, had been on the losing side of the Japanese civil war of 1600. The victorious Tokugawa clan, as was customary in Japan, allowed the Satsuma clan to retain its feudal territories as a *tozama daimyo* (outside lord). However, because of the potential threat that all such *tozama* fiefs held for the victorious faction, close government scrutiny was kept over the Satsuma samurai. Then, by Tokugawa decree, Satsuma was "permitted" to march against the Ryukyu Islands. This was done both to punish Okinawa for refusing to supply Japan with materials needed for her abortive attack on China in 1592, and because the Tokugawa *shogun* feared the armed strength of Satsuma and felt that an overseas "adventure" would be the perfect prescription for soothing the frustrations of Shimazu's warriors.[26] The resulting military expedition in 1609 ended Okinawan independence and made way for complete Satsuma control over all the Ryukyus.

A number of prohibitive ordinances proclaimed by Iehisa Shimazu included a ban on all weapons. Arms found in an Okinawan's possession were immediately confiscated and the owner or holder thereof severely punished. The bitterness that arose from such total subjugation was difficult for many of the islanders to bear in silence, and clashes between the two groups began to occur. In such battles the Okinawans were forced to use the only "weapons" they still possessed, which generally amounted to little more than their bare hands and feet.[27]

Seeing that such disunited resistance was gaining them little, the various Okinawan *ch'uan fa* groups and *tode* societies had a series of secret conferences that resulted in their banding together in 1629 as a united front against the enemy. The result was that a new fighting style developed from this combination of *tode* and *ch'uan fa,* which was simply called *te,* or literally, "hand."[28] This seventeenth-century development is the first recorded instance of an art that closely approximates modern karate. *Te* might be described as the intermediate stage between *tode-ch'uan fa* and karate.

During these early years of development, *te* practice was shrouded in utmost secrecy due to the iron-clad Satsuma edict that was designed to eradicate every trace of the

Okinawan martial arts.[29] The three leading *te* schools—located in Shuri, Naha, and Tomari—went "underground" to avoid detection by the Satsuma samurai. Because of this turn of events, *te* took on two distinctive characteristics: first, it became known as an esoteric art because of the secrecy under which it was taught and practiced; second, it became extremely violent since the sole purpose of its practitioners was to maim or kill. Historically speaking, this going underground had the effect of halting the written chroniclization of the art, and for the next century or so we must again rely on oral traditions. The best verified of these traditions come to us in the form of legends.

One of these legends states that a certain man named Sakugawa from Shuri made a trip to China in 1724 in quest of initiation into the *ch'uan fa* arts. As he was not heard from for many years, his kin thought him lost. But one day, many years later, he reappeared in Shuri, a greatly changed man. His apparent mastery over his body, and the skill with which he performed the extremely complex *ch'uan fa kata* (preset forms), caused many to ask to become his pupils. The result was the now-famed Sakugawa School of karate, which, though termed a "karate school" by the famous Okinawan karate master Gichin Funakoshi,[30] was probably based on pure Chinese *ch'uan fa.*

The second legend important for our purposes is based on another Shuri resident named Shionja. Together with a Chinese master, Kusanku (Japanese pronunciation) with whom he had studied *ch'uan fa* in China, he returned to his home on Okinawa in 1784 after residence abroad. The many disciples who accompanied the pair helped to popularize yet another style of *ch'uan fa.* This incident is recorded in a book entitled *Oshima Hikki,* whose author, a certain Tobe of Tosa village, is said to have obtained the story in detail through a series of interviews with Shionja himself.[31] Aside from these two tales there is little of any

George Miyasaki checks a student's performance of *sanchin*, a breathing *kata* in *Goju-ryu*, a system originating in Naha.

consequence about karate development in even the oral chronology until 1903 when this art was first publicly demonstrated on Okinawa.[32]

Between 1784 and 1903 "karate" replaced "te" as the

term commonly used to designate the major form of Okinawan weaponless fighting. Of course, there were those who preferred using the antiquated terms "te" and "tode," and who have persisted in so doing to the present day. Some writers have even stated that the term "karate" was not known until 1902 or 1903.[33] However, upon interviewing Okinawan immigrants in Hawaii, a karate practitioner was found who had studied karate as a youth in Okinawa as early as 1894, and who knew the art to be called "karate" at that time.[34] Thus, although it is not possible to point with certainty to the time when this term became common in Okinawa, the evidence available indicates that it took place in the latter part of the nineteenth century.

In 1904, karate, written 唐手, was officially introduced into the Okinawan public schools as a regular part of the physical education curriculum.[35] "Karate" thus became a more or less standard term by 1910 and remained so until the "new" ideographs 空手 (see Chap 1, p. 20) replaced the old in approximately 1936.

Okinawan Karate from the Nineteenth Century

It has been almost impossible to tell when the secrecy surrounding karate was relaxed. Several modern karate authorities claim that the intense seclusion of karate was maintained until about 1903.[36] This supposition seems difficult to believe in view of the fact that in 1875 Satsuma's "unofficial" occupation of Okinawa ended and the Ryukyu Islands became officially a part of the Japanese Empire. With Japan's recognition of Okinawa as part of the nation, so to speak, the Okinawan people would seemingly have no further reason for retaining such secrecy. But logic and reality do not always coincide.

One explanation is the fact that secret societies of any

type find it difficult to suddenly change their traditional character. Another explanation lies in the intense rivalry that developed within the karate schools of Naha, Shuri, and Tomari. This rivalry was the result of the all-too-human failing of not being able to adjust to peace after an intense period of war. Since the practitioners of these arts had been trained primarily to kill, they were suddenly faced with a lack of enemies. And so each school began vying with the others for supremacy in these arts.[37]

In most cases, the leaders of the schools did their best to keep the rivalry on the plane of a competitive sport with the goal of teaching pupils to administer quasi-death-dealing blows to one another that were stopped in midair a split second before the lethal physical contact was made. On the other hand, many Okinawan schools preferred to keep their art on a higher level, disdaining competitions of any sort and practicing only the *kata* movements as the means for mastery of their particular style. A few of the present-day Okinawan masters refuse to be swept-up in the sporting elements possible in karate, thus *dan* (grade) ranking, tournaments, or even practice sparring matches within the circle of students is prohibited. In the clubs where competitions became a featured part of training there were naturally many accidents before a set of ironclad rules was worked out, and many hot-tempered individuals failed completely to heed the "new wave" of nonviolence. The unfortunate result was that some karate adherents became labeled as generally unsavory. This tradition has carried through to the present day where, in most Japanese films in which an exponent of karate is depicted, he is invariably portrayed as a villain. Also, since karate is thought of as a "foreign" art (Okinawan), it is easier to make the villain a karateka. Because of these characteristics of karate development, those applying for their admission to a karate school were generally called upon to take rather severe vows of silence and allegiance. This was done so that they would realize the importance of preventing at all cost the secrets they were about to learn from leaking into a rival camp. It is interesting to note that similar precautions were taken in various Hawaiian karate clubs in the past.

We have seen that karate development on Okinawa was limited in scope and popular appeal before 1903. Oral records are responsible for many of the myths and theories of karate development. Since there are virtually no written references to the native art of the Ryukyus (*tode*), the scant information that we have on it is based on oral traditions as well. However, by exploring briefly the development of the ideographs standing for the various art forms associated with karate or its prototypes, we can see some very interesting, tangible occurrences.

Tode is considered indigenous to Okinawa because *ch'uan fa* uses mainly *kaishu* 開手, which refers to open-handed techniques, while *tode* employs the use of the fist technique called *taiso* 太祖.[38] *Taiso* literally means "founder" or "progenitor" and the same characters are sometimes used to represent the founder of the T'ang dynasty (A.D. 618–907) in China. Why a set of ideographs having so much Chinese association would be used to represent the closed-fist style that is thought to be native to Okinawa is a mystery. A possible explanation can be found in Okinawa's longtime role of subservience to China. Until the Satsuma invasion in 1609 there was a constant and influential clique of pro-Chinese advisers to the various Okinawan kings, and Okinawa continued to pay tribute to China even after formal annexation by Japan. It is no wonder that many so-called Okinawan customs have a Chinese "flavor." Linguistically, it is possible that the *tode* pronunciation of the ideographs 唐手 was in existence before *ch'uan fa* played a major role in the culmination of modern karate and that when the Chinese writing system was established on

Okinawa, the Chinese ideographs that phonetically approximated "tode" were written 唐手.

There seems to be a general agreement among contemporary karate authorities that Chinese *ch'uan fa* did play an important part in the development of this fighting art. Modern karate is said to be a combination of closed-fist techniques from Okinawa, finger-thrusting (*nukite*) techniques from Taiwan, open-handed forms from China, and kicking techniques from Southeast Asia.[39]

It was previously explained how the Chinese-Ryukyu Island intercourse developed; however, the routes that the Taiwanese elements of karate took in their migration to Okinawa are not definitely established. Due to the proximity of Taiwan it is possible that direct communication between these two areas resulted in Okinawan adaptation of the Taiwanese finger-thrust. As we saw earlier, there were numerous exchanges between Okinawa, Thailand, and Indochina. Kicking arts may have come direct from Thailand or Indochina or entered the Ryukyu Islands indirectly via Taiwan or Foochow in China.

By way of a summary, karate development in Okinawa can be broken into rather well-defined periods. There was a form of weaponless martial art between A.D. 581–907, which corresponds to the Sui and T'ang dynasties in China; however, the information concerning these eras is scanty and lacking in definitive resource material. From 907 to 1300, there is little information regarding any form of fighting styles. Between 1300 and 1570, which roughly corresponds to the Ming dynasty in China, we find oral traditions concerning *ch'uan fa* and *tode* activity in Okinawa. During the secretive years (1609–1903), we find little information of karate activity, although this was the period of the greatest karate development.

After 1903 karate became more or less standardized in various styles or "ryu," some of which are: *Goju-ryu, Shorin-*

ryu, Shotokan, Shito-ryu, Shindo Jinen-ryu, Wado-ryu, Kushin-ryu, and *Kan-ryu.*[40]

In 1915 karate was officially brought into Japan by Gichin Funakoshi when he demonstrated the art at the great Japanese martial arts headquarters in Kyoto called the Butokuden.[41] During the years following 1915, a number of other famous Okinawan karate masters journeyed to Japan to teach their art, thus formally informing the world abroad that it, too, was deserving of being added to the list of progenitors of an effective and well-developed system of weaponless hand-to-hand combat.

CHAPTER 6 JAPAN

JAPANESE-American relations have gone from the "honeymoon" stage to one of rivalry and so-called "Japan bashing." "Things Japanese" were much in vogue in the two decades following the end of World War II. Americans marveled at Japan's recuperative prowess and hundreds of thousands of American military personnel reveled in the "no sweat" duty in Japan. But in the 1970s Japan began to rival American productivity and in the 1980s and 1990s Japan outdistanced American enterprise with their industrial technology and business drive.

The ugly head of racism has again emerged, and Japan has taken her share of criticism and racial slurs. With all of the press, good and bad, about Japanese-American relations, most

Americans still fail to understand Japanese culture and tradition.

Books dealing with *bu-jutsu* (Japanese martial arts in general) have, particularly in the past few years, glutted the world's "Orientalist" markets. Too many, however, have been written by those who lack the credentials for authorship or who have failed to compile sufficient *apparatus criticus* to support their works. Karate, specifically, has been badly misrepresented because of the innumerable attempts to acquaint the American public with it in the form of a "how-to" sport, or as a means of protecting oneself against the bullies of life. The effect of all this sensationalistic journalism has been that the average reader is pretty well convinced not only that karate was designed primarily as a lethal way of disposing of one's enemies, but also that in its origins it is as Japanese as Shinto, Mt. Fuji, and cherry blossoms.

Japan, though not the birthplace of karate, has had, since hoary antiquity, a tradition of rather exotic military arts. In practice, some of these have an admitted resemblance to modern karate. In Japan's mythological era (before A.D. 500) it is said that the demigods Takeminakata No Kami and Takemikazuchi No Kami engaged in some sort of hand-to-hand combat that the records refer to as a "strength contest."[1] From the depictions of this historical battle, we can infer that they were pitting one weaponless fighting art against another. During this same dawning period of the historical age, another legendary duel occurred between Nomi No Sukune and Taemonokehaya,[2] again with no weapons. References to such contests abound in Japan's early literature dealing with the birth of a unified Japanese nation, and although these tales are couched in the symbolism of Japanese mythology, there is every likelihood that many, if not all, were inspired by actual struggles.

A few writers have noted a similarity between these contests and ju-jutsu (or incorrectly, jiu-jitsu) and sumo wrestling. However, closer scrutiny indicates that the type of fighting depicted more nearly resembles what is currently thought of as karate. But at this point great care in drawing conclusions must be exercised. We are by no means implying that karate per se so existed in ancient Japan. The system of movements called karate is, as we have seen, an eclectic art that reached its culmination in the Ryukyu Islands. The possibility does exist, however, that a type of *ch'uan fa* found its way into early Japan and that it was instrumental in the formation of other martial arts.

Early Chinese Influences

Japan became enamored with China and Chinese culture as early as A.D. 607 when the first official Japanese embassy was sent to China. This event served to establish formal relations between the eastern islanders and the Sui dynasty rulers.[3] For several centuries thereafter a continuous flow of Chinese ideas entered the Japanese islands. The official intercourse between the two nations ceased after A.D. 894, but unofficial relations existed through the twelfth century.[4] After this date a satiation point was reached and Japan isolated her frontiers, except for occasional Zen priests who journeyed between the nations. Today, Chinese influence is apparent in Japan's written language, art, architecture, religion, and in numerous subtleties of culture and etiquette, though the overt suggestion of this to many native Japanese will evoke an indignant denial. From the point of view of the student of martial arts, however, the Sinification of Japan is regarded as singularly far reaching, and thus must be studied with great care.

We cannot, on the other hand, subscribe to the theories

of those who assert that the *bu-jutsu* of Japan are the direct result of Chinese influence and inspiration. Although such arts as *kempo* (*ch'uan fa*), sumo, *yawara, torite, ashikeri, ken-jutsu,* and ju-jutsu could have drifted across the waterways from China at unrecorded times,[5] such a hypothesis seems untenable when viewed in the harsh light of existing facts. It may be concluded that while China was a focal point that radiated "culture" to the outside "barbarian" world, many of the aforementioned Japanese *bu-jutsu* had their beginnings in the Japanese islands exclusively.

Buddhism, the great continental philosophy, was first brought to Japan by bands of Chinese and Korean travelers[6] in the sixth century. With the founding of China's T'ang dynasty in A.D. 608, there began a period of close Chinese contacts. The resulting flow of ideas from the mainland served to firmly implant this embryonic religion in the Japanese nation, largely through the efforts of peripatetic Buddhist priests who moved back and forth freely between the two countries. Thus at the same time that its power and influence was beginning to spread to Japan, Buddhism in China was at its zenith in popularity.

In Chapter 5 the theory was advanced that the Buddhist monks among various shipwrecked castaway groups had inadvertently brought a weaponless self-defense system to the Ryukyu Islands. It follows then, that, if mere accidents resulted in Okinawa's learning a Chinese weaponless martial art, the volitional residence of such Buddhist priests in Japan points rather certainly to exchanges of ideas on such techniques. Thus, there is every likelihood that the neophyte Japanese priests were taught a form of self-defense for use during their travels.

Records, travel diaries, and similar chronicles showing the routes and general histories of these early priests have never been fully analyzed—in many instances never having been seen at all by Western historians. Voluminous written materials exist in Japanese Buddhist monasteries that are generally unavailable to the laity, and even more documents exist in remote Chinese Buddhist and Taoist temples. Aside from the general lack of access to this valuable data, a researcher in this area must be proficient in three of the world's more esoteric and difficult languages: classical Chinese, archaic Japanese, and Indian Sanskrit. So few researchers have the requisite combination of access and language mastery that it would seem that these mysteries will remain forever unsolved. Moreover, almost all of the academicians possessing the scholarly and language capabilities necessary for study of Asian cultures have neglected the more mundane subject of military arts. This is primarily the reason why most references dealing with Asia simply refer to the assorted Oriental fighting techniques as "pugilism" or "wrestling."

A further theory exists that during the seventh and fourteenth centuries, when it was common for Japanese youths to study Buddhism in China, they learned *ch'uan fa* along with their studies and brought knowledge of this art back to their homeland.[7] Since, as we pointed out, there are such close ties between *ch'uan fa* and Buddhist philosophy, this hypothesis is far from being an extreme statement.

In the Heian period (A.D. 794–1185) Buddhist monasteries used armed bands to settle local disputes,[8] and there are enigmatic reports of priests of rival temples clashing with such violence in the streets of Heian-kyo (Kyoto), that government intervention was needed to preserve order.[9]

During the classical age of Japanese martial arts (*ca.* 1500–1868) the leading *bu-jutsu* men were often Buddhist monks, and they regularly displayed special knowledge and skill in unarmed forms of fighting. In fact, *ch'uan fa* (pronounced "KEM-po" in Japanese) was not known by many people outside of the Buddhist priesthood until the latter part of the sixteenth century.

In 1592 Hideyoshi Toyotomi, the great warlord general of Japan, effected his plan for the complete conquest of China. With the transporting of his tremendous army to Korea, the campaign, which was to involve Japan in an overseas invasion for the next six years, was begun. So fierce was the combined Korean-Chinese resistance that in 1598, when Hideyoshi died, the tattered remnants of his army returned home without ever setting foot on Chinese soil. Rather, the Korean isthmus was the unfortunate site of the many clashes between the opposing military factions, and emerged from Japan's first foreign "adventure" a devastated land.

In Japanese oral tradition it is recorded that many of Hideyoshi's returning samurai brought with them a working knowledge of *ch'uan fa* and that from the sixteenth century onward, part of the samurai's "armament" included a punching and nerve-striking technique based on Chinese *ch'uan fa.*

The relationship of Chinese military arts to the rise of a Japanese system of weaponless self-defense is vague and not fully documented by reliable sources. We do have one accurate date, however, that is authenticated by competent historians. In 1638, during the Tokugawa period, a Chinese pottery master named Ch'en Yuan-pin (1587–1671) arrived from China to serve as a ceramics instructor for the *daimyo* (lord) of Owari.[10] Among his other duties, Ch'en instructed several *ronin* (masterless samurai) in the art of seizing a man without the use of weapons.[11] Some sources have even credited this man with the introduction of *ch'uan fa* and ju-jutsu into the Japanese islands.[12] Because of its precise date, this story is popularly circulated as the beginning of a karate-like art in Japan. Yet, knowledgeable historians will dispute this theory on the grounds that a weaponless technique called *yawara* was in existence long before Ch'en came to Japan.[13] *Yawara,* it seems, is the precursor to a form of ju-jutsu and is believed by many Japanese writers to be the earliest prototype of a native bare-handed fighting art, though in some forms of *yawara* a pocket stick is used. Little else is known about this art and it remains one of the most esoteric of all the existing Japanese *bu-jutsu.* Thus, although Ch'en Yuan-pin is a very real and documented individual, his entry into the field of weaponless arts came well after their establishment as an integral part of Japan's military arts. Jigoro Kano, the founder of modern judo, stated in 1888 that of the various arts instrumental in judo's development, ju-jutsu played the most vital role.[14] Professor Kano stated conclusively that the Chinese form of fighting without weapons (i.e., *ch'uan fa)* differs so radically from ju-jutsu that there is no chance of their interconnection, and that therefore the leverage and seizing arts are of Japanese origin.[15]

Japanese Martial Arts in the Twentieth Century

Although Okinawan karate "officially" entered Japan with the famous Gichin Funakoshi in 1915, several Okinawan karate instructors are known to have traveled and taught in Japan as early as 1904. Full-scale public initiation to the art occurred in 1915 when Master Funakoshi demonstrated karate before a large assembly of interested Japanese spectators at the Butokuden in Kyoto. Thus, although karate-like styles of fighting came to Japan during the period of heavy Buddhist contacts from China with Hideyoshi's returning armies in the sixteenth century, and again with Ch'en Yuan-pin in the seventeenth century, 1915 stands as the established date of Okinawan karate's entry into the Japanese islands.

After the impetus of 1915, karate developed rather slowly into a fully accepted Japanese *bu-jutsu.* A number of promi-

University students in Japan training on the *makiwara* (striking post).

nent karate masters (e.g., Chojun Miyagi, Choki Motobu, etc.) from the Ryukyus secured teaching assignments as instructors of karate at a few of Japan's most notable universities.

The aforementioned Chojun Miyagi lectured and taught his art at Kyoto Imperial University in 1928.[16] In 1932 Miyagi became a "coach" in the newly formed karate department of Kansai University in Osaka, often lecturing to karate and boxing clubs located throughout the city.[17] Thus, by the time war reached the Japanese citizenry on a universal scale in 1937, karate had received a general introduction to the populace as a whole, but was much more of an integral part of both university and military life. So much so, in fact, that by the end of World War II, karate had become a special part of the secondary and college campus scene. However, the real period of karate interest, as we shall see, began in the years following World War II.

The entry of karate into Japan in the early twentieth century started a new era in Japanese *bu-jutsu.* Many "new" forms of martial ways appeared that had evolved from traditional styles. One of the most famous of these was aikido.

Morihei Uyeshiba developed aikido after World War II. Having mastered kendo and ju-jutsu in his youth, Uyeshiba felt that there could be an art designed to control one's ambitions and desires along with martial training. He claimed his art was primarily a vehicle to enlightenment.[18]Aikido does not employ brute strength, nor does it teach strikes and kicks. Under Uyeshiba, this art is purely defensive and there are no competitive contests.[19]As an exercise and philosophical medium, aikido is like ta'i chi ch'uan.

CHAPTER 7
KOREA

KOREA LOOMS out of the mists of antiquity as one of the most ancient and enigmatic countries on earth. Recorded history of Korea does not begin until the Christian era; however, Korean oral history places its foundation in the third millennium B.C. In 1122 B.C., a kingdom called Choson was founded by a Chinese exile named Kija in North Korea. Han dynasty China ended Korean independence in the second century B.C., and from this period until modern times, Korea suffered countless foreign invasions.

The effect of foreign influence on the development of Korean martial arts will never be fully known. It seems that the histories of all the nations examined in this study show eclecticism as much as invention. Be that as it may,

Korea did develop a fighting art that just may be the most widely practiced martial art in the world today.

Hundreds of millions of people worldwide witnessed on television over a thousand martial artists demonstrating in the opening ceremonies for the 1988 Summer Olympics in Seoul, Korea. The art exhibited was tae kwon do (tay-kwan-dough, which means, "the way of kicking and punching"), and what makes this remarkable is the fact that the name tae kwon do did not exist until 1955.[1] This rather late burgeoning was due to secrecy of the practitioners, a common story in Asian martial arts, and numerous historical events in Korean history that slowed consolidation of martial arts styles until the postwar period.

Of course 1955 was not the birthdate for tae kwon do. Its precursors go back into antiquity. This can be readily seen when one examines the geography of Korea. This peninsular country lies between China and Japan, and has long been a buffer between these two great powers. Not unlike Poland, Korea, as previously stated, has seen numerous invaders come and go, bringing a wide assortment of religious, artistic, and military knowledge.

The "Hermit Kingdom," as Korea was called in the West, never fully developed a bladed weapons culture and system of sword fighting like China, and especially Japan. However, there was an art of sword making but it should be classified as artistic rather than functional. Designs included straight swords, double-edged swords, and those inlaid with precious gems; they were prized as works of art.[2]

Korea was on the periphery of China and Manchuria and hence came under the general suzerainty of these two regions from time to time. However, the Korean people had a fierce independent spirit, and in their minds, Korea was an independent nation, though there were periods when it was conquered territorially if not spiritually.

Many Koreans feel that tae kwon do is the eclectic evolution of native forms of fighting that go back into antiquity. As an early means of protecting oneself from human and animal enemies, a form of fighting was developed called *subak* (sometimes *soo bahk)*, dating as early as the Koguryo dynasty (37 B.C.–668 A.D.).[3] The evidence for this claim is to be found in mural paintings on the walls of the royal tombs of Myong Chong and Kak Chu Chong in what is now Chinese Manchuria.[4] By the time of the fall of the Chinese Han dynasty (*ca.* 220 A.D.), the Korean kingdom of Koguryo occupied most of North Korea and nearly all of what is now south Manchuria.[5] The combatants in the paintings are wearing loincloths and seem to be using a bare-handed form of fighting.[6] In some of these cave frescos and murals the fighters depicted closely resemble Mongol wrestlers.[7]

Of course we need to understand that all ancient forms of bare-handed fighting show similarities; it must be understood that temple paintings and statuary do not form conclusive evidence of the existence of one fighting form over another, nor do they prove that the stances and postures of the figures represent anything unique and distinctive. It is therefore possible to see what the observer wants to see in any figure of a person in some kind of stance, whether it is combative, dancelike, etc.

Korea came under Chinese control in the second century B.C., creating an infusion of Chinese *ch'uan fa.*[8] This aided the development of Korean martial arts, but it was by no means the only impetus. Some Korean martial artists even claim that wandering monks from the famous Shaolin Monastery in China brought into Korea the essence of bare-handed fighting and Buddhist philosophical teachings. This combination (with sprinklings of Confucianism and Taoism) is a common feature of all Korean martial arts.[9] Groups of Korean people, in what might be described as "tribes" or "clans," developed outside of the Chinese sphere of influence. These tribes came to form the three kingdoms of Paekche (also spelled Baekje), Silla, and the aforementioned Koguryo.[10] Silla (57 B.C.–935 A.D.) was a kingdom in the southern part of Korea that was noted for its stone Buddhist carvings, some of which show martial arts stances.[11]

Paekche appears to have been the weakest of the three kingdoms; however, some writers claim that Paekche harbored a martial arts tradition.[12] Other writers disagree claiming its people gravitated away from the martial arts and towards religious studies.[13] Regardless, Buddhism flourished, with temple building and religious art in the forefront of Paekche's creativity.[14] With Chinese help, Silla destroyed Paekche in the fourth century A.D. The feuding of the three kingdoms for sole control of the land led to widespread destruction all over Korea.

Civil war finally ended when the kingdom of Silla became dominant in the Korean peninsula during the latter part of the seventh century. From this date to 935, Silla ruled Korea in what was later called "the Golden Age."

Development During the Silla, Koryo, and Yi Dynasties

During Silla's reign a military order developed called the "Flowering Knights" or *Hwarang*.[15] Their purpose was to generate moral and patriotic ideals among select Korean noblemen.[16] The *Hwarang* often visited famous mountains because of the spiritual connection therein; they also celebrated ritual songs and dances as a form of prayer for military victories.[17] Some of the tenets of the "Flowering Knights" were in a philosophical code called *Hwarang-do*, which includes:

1. Loyalty to the King
2. Faithfulness to one's friend

3. Devotion to one's parents
4. Bravery and absolute obedience on the battlefield
5. A prohibition against wanton killing of any form of life[18]

The first three tenets are more closely related to Confucian ethics than Buddhism. It should be noted that the *Hwarang-do* is a moral code and does not emphasize a combat technique or fighting style.[19] The *Hwarang* spread their influence all through the peninsula and excelled in archery and unarmed combat. Between the months of July and August, an annual national festival was conducted whereby the *Hwarang* could demonstrate their martial skill.[20] One of the major reasons Silla was able to win control over Paekche and Koguryo in the unification war of 668 was the military skill of the *Hwarang*.[21] Many myths were recorded during the reign of Silla. With the introduction of written Chinese and later the hangul system of writing the Korean language, folk tales were written down. In a work called *The Memorabilia of the Three Kingdoms* (*Samguk Sagi* and *Samguk Yusa*), exploits of the *Hwarang* were chronicled for the people to read about.[22] During the period of 634–653 A.D., two queens of the Silla court developed relations with the T'ang Chinese court; they also sponsored the sending of Korean students to China for the purpose of learning Chinese warfare.[23]

In 935 A.D. the Koryo dynasty was founded. This dynastic succession continued the martial arts tradition created by Korea's warlike past and popularized it so that it gained widespread acceptance among the common people.[24] Wang Kyon, as founder of the Koryo, systematized and began instructing the Korean military in *subak*. One of its most famous exponents was the commander-in-chief to the sixteenth King, Ui Jong.[25] *Subak* was highlighted in an annual combat tournament held in May and participation by soldiers was mandatory; the winner could be given an important government post, and three such champions actually became generals of the armed forces.[26]

Up to the decline of the Koryo dynasty, most martial arts practitioners were either nobles or soldiers. The general populace did not practice the "systematized" forms of combat in large numbers, though they did have fighting arts for self-defense. It was in the Yi dynasty (1392–1910) that a book was written about *subak* that elevated this art from a sporting craft to a martial art.[27] This ended the military's monopoly on *subak* and "gave it to the people."[28]

The Yi dynasty held learning and scholarship in very high esteem, and Confucianism replaced Buddhism as the state religion. During the nearly five centuries of the Yi, interest in the martial arts declined. However, during this period two training manuals were published on martial arts showing twenty-four fighting techniques,[29] and the term *tae kyon* was used for the first time to describe these arts.[30]

In what seems to be a sterile period of development in any art, often there results some significant transition or improvement. *Tae kyon* was not defunct or forgotten. It continued to flourish in private academies much as *ch'uan fa* did as the fighting art of the various Chinese secret societies. This even more so when Japan ended Korean independence in 1910.

Korean Martial Arts in the Twentieth Century

When Japan gained control of Korea in 1910, it was not their first invasion of that country. The most aggressive sojourn into Korea before the twentieth century occurred in 1592, when the warlord Hideyoshi ravaged the peninsula for seven years. Driven out because of several brilliant Korean naval victories, including the first-ever use of an ironclad ship, Hideyoshi's army returned to Japan. However, Korea continued to be viewed for conquest.

Without going into the political intrigues that brought on Japanese control in 1910, the martial arts historian needs only to understand how the Japanese control of Korea brought about more systems of fighting. Japan outlawed the native Korean forms, but allowed Koreans access to such Japanese *bu-jutsu* as kendo, judo, and ju-jutsu. Of course, this was done only under strict Japanese control. But herein lies the development of the other major Korean fighting art, *hapkido*.

Shortly after Japan's occupation, Yong Suhl Choi, a *tae kyon* master, emigrated to Japan. There Choi studied *Daito-*

Jeff Harris performs a *hapkido* throw.

ryu ju-jutsu, a forerunner of judo and aikido.[31] Master Choi remained in Japan and perfected his "throwing" art, which is based on ju-jutsu and judo, and returned to Korea at the end of World War II.[32] He founded the first *hapkido* school in Taegu, South Korea. His art is a mix of *tae kyon* and Japanese ju-jutsu, making it a unique blend of the "hard" *tae kyon* forms and the "soft" throwing art of ju-jutsu.[33] The term *hapkido* is made up of three words: "hap," meaning harmony or coordination; "ki," meaning power or "cosmic force," and "do," indicating the "way."[34] These are the same three characters used in the word "aikido" in Japanese.

Also after World War II we see the birth of tae kwon do. During the Japanese occupation (1910–1945) many Koreans studied Japanese karate. The techniques they learned were, in some instances, only slightly modified when adopted into the Korean arts after W.W.II.[35] This brought about a series of names for "Korean" forms, namely *kong soo* (empty hand), *tang soo* (T'ang hand),[36] and *hwa soo* (*Hwarang* hand). In 1955, the title tae kwon do was officially adopted.[37]

The name tae kwon do was confirmed by a consensus of Korean martial arts masters, some of whom were returning to Korea after World War II with many new techniques taken from Chinese, Okinawan, and Japanese martial arts.[38] The actual term "tae kwon do" was suggested by Master Hong Hi Choi.[39] As they say, the rest in history. Tae kwon do is now taught in all levels of the Korean school system, and is a requisite for military training. Tae kwon do has spread overseas to almost every country and it is one of the few Asian martial arts that has a true world championship. It has been a demonstration sport in the 1988 and 1992 Olympics and there is good reason to believe it will be an official sport in the 1996 games.

Korea, then, has produced two major martial arts forms: tae kwon do and *hapkido*. The inevitable question that comes up in any discussion of martial arts is, which system is superior? Tae kwon do is called a "hard style" where kicking is about seventy-five percent of the techniques and punching the other twenty-five percent. The body in tae kwon do is somewhat rigid or flexed so that blows can be warded off and punches and kicks delivered with maximum force. *Hapkido*, on the other hand, is called a "soft" style, where leverage and balance are keys to throwing and/or subduing the opponent. This is where its origins in Japanese aikido and ju-jutsu become readily apparent. On balance, the effectiveness of both arts would depend on the ability of the performer and his psychological and physiological gravitation. As in any of the arts mentioned herein, the quality of the practitioner is the most important factor.

In closing, when established historical hypotheses are challenged, the term "revisionist" is often a term given to the author of such works. It is a label that more often than not denotes criticism. For anyone who dares to say that Korean martial arts are not indigenous to that peninsula since hoary antiquity runs this risk of being called a "revisionist." One suspects that the Korean martial arts establishment would find much stronger words to criticize anyone varying from the "accepted" theories.

Two non-Korean researchers have published such findings: Willy Pieter and Robert W. Young, both in *The Journal of Asian Martial Arts*. They say that most so-called Korean martial arts are not original creations.[40] They claim that some are probably Chinese in origin but most date from the years of Japanese occupation.[41]

Whether such historical contradictions will ever be sorted out to everyone's satisfaction is undoubtedly out of the realm of possibility. But a serious student of the Korean martial arts should be aware of the controversy. Whether ancient or a product of modern eclecticism, tae kwon do, *et. al.* are effective fighting arts that rightfully stand alongside the other great Asian martial arts.

CHAPTER 8

BUDDHISM AND KARATE

仏教

THERE HAS long been a trend among karatephiles to associate karate with Buddhist philosophy. Some writers have stated categorically that the two are inseparable. We will examine the available facts in order to see whether such a hypothesis is tenable.

An inspection of the ideograph that represents the *kara* 空 portion of "karate" reveals an apparent linguistic relationship to Buddhism,[1] since the same ideograph in Buddhism represents the "void," or *sunyata*. *Sunyata*, the Sanskrit term for "emptiness" or "nothingness," is used to represent the ancient metaphysical concept that all basic principles of life emanate from within an infinite and pristine chaos. This capsulized definition, depending on how each of its constituent terms is defined, demonstrates the fact that *sunyata* virtually defies definition even when one's tools comprise the entire English language. With this conclusion most contemporary Buddhist philosophers agree. However, in contradistinction to their avowed dislike of such definitions, many of these same Buddhist writers and theologians have made attempts at describing and categorizing *sunyata,* such that we find an exceedingly rich and varied body of interpretations.

One of the most often cited of these interpretations takes us deep into hoary Indian antiquity. In the second century, Nagarjuna, one of Buddhism's most revered patriarchs, set forth *sunyata* as: "The nature of reality, or rather, of the conceptions of reality that the human mind can form."[2] Nagarjuna's idea *of sunyata* was that all things are relative and without self-nature, and that the only things that can be considered concrete or as possessing absolute properties are those that are related to other things. This is the concept of "relevance," one of the most complex of all Buddhist philosophical ideas. A complete summation of its manifold ramifications fills many volumes; and because of its esoteric nature it is generally found only in Buddhist canons.

Those scholars who link karate with *sunyata* often rely on the phase known as "nothingness," saying, in effect, that karate is a weaponless—and therefore empty-handed—art, and that it becomes a concrete "entity" only when the body is applied to the various moves and gestures that constitute the karate attack and defense repertoire. Another example of this principle is that when attacked by an aggressor, the genuine karate practitioner responds with what amounts to reflex action. Such reflex is supposedly without volition, and is therefore, as the claim goes, "relative" in the Buddhist sense of *sunyata.*

It is, of course, self-evident that the term "karate" is an abstraction having no "self-nature" or "substance," and remains so until its principles are transformed into body movements. However, care must certainly be exercised in drawing analogies from such abstrusions so that they remain within the bounds of logical derivation and do not become mere mental gymnastics. For example, it should be noted that many Buddhist concepts can be applied to any number of actions in the exterior world of the senses. And as regards karate in particular we certainly cannot discount the well-corroborated fact that the "kara" portion of "karate," as it is presently written, did not come into use until about 1936, the ramifications of which we will explore in this chapter. Whether or not early *ch'uan fa* masters in China or *tode*-karate masters on Okinawa were genuinely preoccupied with Buddhist philosophy remains at the time of this writing a matter of speculation.

A recent trend among writers in the general field of Asian martial arts has been to tie in certain aspects of Buddhism with specific sporting and military techniques. The *mu* principle of Buddhism is an example of this, having been associated with both judo and kendo for a number of years. *Mu* literally means "nothing," and as such bears a cursory resemblance to the concept of *sunyata.* But after more careful philological research, one finds that *mu* more specifically refers to nonstriving or nonseeking, a tie-in with Sakyamuni's doctrine of the "middle path" of no extremes rather than with *sunyata.* In judo the *mu* principle is applied when two opponents face each other before a match, the idea being to clear the mind of extraneous thoughts rather than to think about the approaching contest. If one is successful, it is claimed that his body responds perfectly from moment to moment. When observing high-ranking judoka perform, those who are aware of this concept claim that they can see it in action, and that facial expression is usually the signpost that indicates whether or not the *mu* concept is being utilized.

The *mu* principle undoubtedly comes from the older Buddhist concept of *mushin,* or "no-mind," that, incidentally, was a special form of Zen training used by the samurai of feudal Japan.[3] In essence, *mushin* is an egoless state of the mind that frees one from fear of death or failure. Musashi Miyamoto (1584–1645), one of the great fencing masters of the Tokugawa period, expressed the idea of *mushin* in the art of *ken-jutsu* (fencing):

> Under the sword lifted high
> There is hell making you tremble;
> But go ahead
> And you have the land of bliss. [4]

A further fact from which one might conclude that karate and Buddhism are interrelated is that most countries possessing a karate-like art are either predominantly Buddhist or have had strong Buddhist influences during their development (e.g., India, Indonesia, Korea, and Okinawa). Aside from the many coincidences of the art and the religion in the same country, there is little direct evidence to show that karate or its related fighting arts throughout Asia developed in direct association with Buddhism. The Bodhidharma "legend" appears to be the only clear-cut exception to this statement.

Bodhidharma and Buddhism in China

Bodhidharma is considered to be the founder of a school of weaponless fighting called Shaolin *ch'uan fa,* the art from which karate derived many of its techniques. This theory, however, raises a number of questions. For example, Bodhidharma's chief concern was apparently to "cultivate" the mind so that enlightenment could be

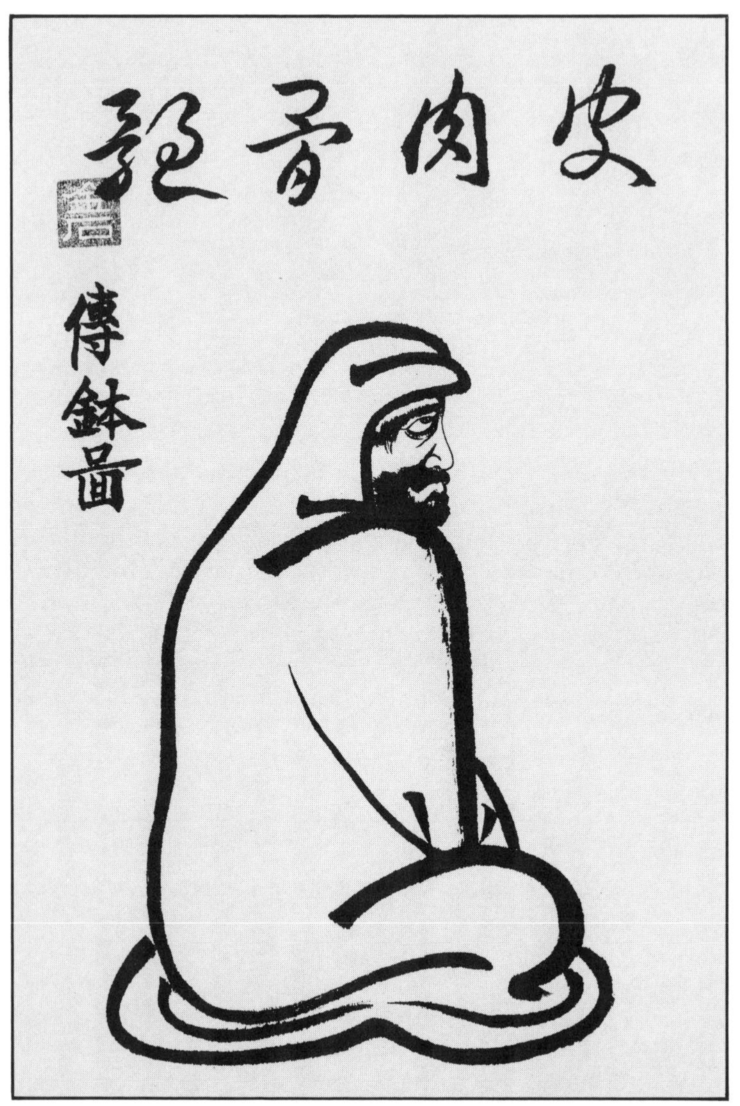

Bodhidharma, the Indian monk who introduced Zen to China.

achieved. It is therefore not at all unusual that he developed a system of calisthenics designed to build physical and mental vitality and to aid in the development of the power of concentration. From these special exercises, called *Shihpa Lohan Shou,* evolved the Shaolin *ch'uan fa.* Because of this link with a Buddhist monk, *ch'uan fa* in general and the Shaolin school in particular can be said to have been Buddhist inspired.

Bodhidharma's main historical significance, however, is on a different level altogether. His roles, both as the twenty-eighth patriarch after Sakyamuni (the historic Buddha) and as the first patriarch of Zen Buddhism in China, are unchallenged by most historians. Bodhidharma entered China in the sixth century, at which time Chinese civilization was already over two thousand years old. At that time the Chinese had a religious "orientation" called Taoism that, in its content and philosophy, already bore a remarkable resemblance to the teachings that Bodhidharma came to enunciate. Though Bodhidharma is generally referred to as the "founder" of Zen in China, a Chinese monk called Hui Neng (638–713) was the real father of Chinese Zen (known as *Ch'an* in Mandarin after the Sanskrit *Dhyana).*[5] Bodhidharma's Indian Zen seemingly could not divorce itself from the lofty metaphysics so characteristic of the bulk of Indian philosophy, and thus failed to impact upon the Chinese mind as he had hoped. On the other hand, Hui Neng introduced a Zen philosophy that was closely akin to Chinese thinking and culture. An explication of the differences involved would necessitate a volume in itself. And, though no capsulized description of Taoism or Zen could hope to explain their myriad complexities, for purposes of brevity it can be said that they are, in essence, paths to "immediate awakening" or "total spiritual insight."[6]

We have seen earlier that Bodhidharma's principal concern was with cultivating the mind so that enlightenment could be achieved. The eighteen-stroke exercise that he taught was certainly not designed for physical confrontation. Likewise, Taoism is never violent, since its ends are achieved "by noninterference (*wu-wei*), which is a kind of psychological judo."[7] Judging from all of the foregoing evidence, one must surely question statements that assert that lethal martial arts like *ch'uan fa* and karate are inextricably interconnected with Zen and Taoism! The fact, simply stated, is that *ch'uan fa* in its inception was not a lethal art, since it was a close blood relative of Bodhidharma's Shaolin *ch'uan fa.*

And then there are those who categorize the whole Bodhidharma story as mere legend. But even if we refute the legend theory and insist on Bodhidharma's historical reality, the continued influence of Buddhism on *ch'uan fa* after his death remains highly questionable. It has until now, for example, been impossible to determine whether Ch'ueh Yuan Shang-jen and Li-shao (the two *ch'uan fa* masters responsible for enlarging the *Shihpa Lohan Shou* after the passing of Bodhidharma) had any Buddhist affiliations. It is further impossible to tell whether or not these two masters would have perpetuated any Buddhist teachings even if they had been acquainted with Bodhidharma's philosophical teachings. In fact, since Ch'ueh and Li were not contemporaries of Bodhidharma—the latter having died *ca.* A.D. 534 and the former two having lived in the Sui dynasty (A.D. 581–618)—it is difficult to determine just how much exposure there was to Bodhidharma's Buddhism, and thus how perfectly they mastered the strict Shaolin *ch'uan fa* discipline.

Another question about the Bodhidharma "legend" stems from the fact that *ch'uan fa is* sometimes said to have flourished in China long before Bodhidharma's advent.[8] We noted in Chapter 3 the tradition stating that *ch'uan fa* originated some three thousand years before the Christian era, during the reign of the Yellow Emperor, Huang-ti.[9] If true, then it would appear that *ch'uan fa* antedates Buddhism and that there would be separate developmental patterns, even though they both originated in India.

The traditional date for the entry of Buddhism into China is the first century B.C. However, significant cultural influences were not seen until about A.D. 220, at which time Buddhism's popularity was largely restricted to the merchant and lower classes.[10] The subsequent development of Buddhism in Chinese society is complex, and while the subject is interesting, it is not properly within the scope of this work. It is enough to say that at this period of development, China, which was called the "Middle Kingdom," was notably hostile to foreign influences. The Chinese considered their culture superior to those "barbarian" cultures of the outside world. From this historical fact alone we can understand why the peripatetic Buddhist monks from India were for so long treated as inferiors by the Chinese gentry.[11]

But with the persistence of ever-increasing numbers of proselytizing monks, Buddhism made steady inroads into China's culture so that by the fourth century, it was solidly entrenched. During the T'ang dynasty (A.D. 618–907), Buddhism reached its pinnacle, and conversely, its ebb during the period's latter years primarily because of the increasing rivalry and strength of Taoism. Buddhism never regained the impetus it had been developing up to that time. Since the majority of the currently active *ch'uan fa* schools in China cannot be historically traced further than the Southern Sung dynasty (1127–1279),[12] it does not seem likely that Buddhism, which lost imperial favor during the latter T'ang dynasty, could be considered closely linked with *ch'uan fa* development. In all subsequent dynasties, Buddhism played rather minor roles, but never entirely dropped from sight. The most recent example came at the end of the Ch'ing dynasty (1644–1912), when Buddhist groups openly engaged in the rebellion against the foreign Manchu rulers. And, though the Buddhist numbers were small in comparison with the Taoist elements similarly engaged, they were outstanding in their effectiveness and were most noted for the great prowess shown by several famous monks who participated openly.

Immediately prior to the Boxer Rebellion in 1900, the leader of the Boxers, Ts'ao Fu T'ien, announced that he had received a decree from the mythical Taoist deity known as the Jade Emperor to oust the barbarians from China.[13] This is significant mainly because it showed the strength of the Taoist philosophy in Chinese political life. Taoism through the centuries had evolved, like so many other religions in the world, by a constant modification of doctrines. By 1900 the traditionally philosophical Taoism that had so strongly influenced the development of Chinese Zen Buddhism had gradually given way to a popular form of Taoism that featured an array of gods, demigods, alchemy, astrology, and other mystical practices. Ts'ao Fu T'ien's pronouncement was just such a mystical feature of contemporary "popular" Taoism. The invocation of the Jade Emperor by a leader of the Boxers indicated that Taoism had permeated the thinking of this revolutionary group, as in fact it had permeated most facets of Chinese society. Also, we saw in Chapter 3 that *ch'uan fa* practice was responsible for the term "Boxers." Since Taoism was the spiritual overtone of this semireligious Western purge, it appears that *ch'uan fa,* the art, was inextricably involved with Taoism, the religion.

Thus even if one were to assume that Buddhism had played a role in the development of *ch'uan fa* philosophy, it must be concluded that it had given nearly all of its ground to Taoism by the late nineteenth or early twentieth century.

Zen and Karate

Unlike the Chinese, who had largely restricted the practice of Buddhism to a monastic society of monks and lay people, the Japanese readily accepted it—particularly Zen Buddhism—into all strata of their society. Zen initially came to the Japanese islands during the Kamakura period (1185–1336). During this epic era of political change in Japan many great Zen masters ruled the entire spiritual hierarchy of Japanese religious circles.[14] The samurai class in particular found Zen expression and "flavor" to their liking. It became the belief that the mastery of any of the military arts began with a foundation in Zen tenets, and that a warrior could not achieve mastery of his art without a period of dedicated Zen training. At the same time, violent death was an ever-present threat to the samurai. Practice in the meditative aspects of Zen gave them a sense of freedom from the fear of life then lived.

Zen influence in the daily lives of the Japanese populace is most markedly seen in the widely practiced art forms such as tea ceremony, flower arranging, landscaping and gardening, painting, archery, and fencing. From this list it can be seen that subtle features of Japanese life reflect Zen influence; but it is the martial arts that have retained the direct, forthright path to enlightenment that was introduced by Bodhidharma. It is this very directness that has led the many thinkers to consider martial arts as a catalyst, or "middle man," between self and universal knowledge, or enlightenment.

In Chapter 2 we briefly explored the thesis that certain forms of Asian art are related to karate, as evidenced by the postures of ancient statues and friezes. The *Nio Bodhisattva* of Japan, the famous guardian deity seen at the gates to many Buddhist temples, appears to be the closest facsimile of a type of *ch'uan fa,* and although the Japanese sculptures depicting fighting positions are the most common today, earlier Chinese and Indian works were the prototypes for these statues. Much of the Buddhist art in China was influenced by Graeco-Buddhist art of Northern India. A general classification of art found in China, Korea, and Japan during the T'ang dynasty is termed the "T'ang-Nara-Silla" style. Since the Buddhist statues of the Japanese pre-Nara period (before 646 A.D.) are based on Indo-Sino styles and since these works show distinct fighting positions, we have still further proof that some variety of *ch'uan fa* was practiced in ancient India and China. Although this fact may be coincidental, it also remains in consideration as an example of Buddhist influence on martial art development in China and Japan.

Since at least the seventh century, Buddhist monks in China and Japan have learned a type of *ch'uan fa* or *kempo.* On the surface it appears that such "defensive techniques" could possess no great religious significance, particularly since their original ancestor—Bodhidharma's *Shihpa Lohan Shou*—is said to have been designed primarily for healthful exercise. But the idea keeps arising that *ch'uan fa* or *kempo* were in actuality forms of "moving meditation,"or aids in achieving enlightenment, which is the goal of every serious Buddhist. Although there are no authoritative sources that can be cited in support of this assumption, this is a valid conclusion from the scraps of evidence—mostly from informants' oral testimony—that were sifted through. It should be made clear, however, that while the moral emphasis found in contemporary karate schools is usually Buddhist in flavor, this remnant is but a small thread of the magnificent fabric of Oriental culture. The quasi-Buddhist philosophy being preached by many karate schools generally approaches the point of blasphemy when it is contrasted with the physical violence and animal aggression that are subtly encouraged therein.

Karate's entry into Japan with Master Funakoshi in 1915 was much too late for it to be considered an integral part of Japan's martial arts or for it to be considered "Zen influenced." Granted, Buddhist monks and Hideyoshi's samurai did bring into Japan a form of *ch'uan fa*. This art, however, did not reach the general masses as its practice was largely restricted to the monastic Buddhist sects and the military class.

It was not until 1936 that a council of karate masters meeting on Okinawa decided to use the "kara" ideograph for writing "karate." It is claimed that they did so because the ideograph was spiritually significant, yet this explanation loses much of its credibility when one realizes that Buddhism had never achieved significant popularity among the Okinawans. In fact, it had never been a particularly strong force in the development of spiritual thought patterns in the Ryukyus, which have been "animistic" since paleolithic times. Thus it appears that the linking of Buddhism with karate is a modern innovation, and is an attempt, perhaps, to give to a deadly fighting technique the vestiges of a moral conscience.

国

CHAPTER 9

KARATE IN THE UNITED STATES

THE FIRST eight chapters have described the formation and evolution of the fighting art called "karate." It has been established that the art is the exclusive property of Asia, Asia in its broadest sense. In fact, there is no good evidence that Western civilization has contributed to any Asian forms of unarmed combat, with the possible exception of Thai boxing where, barring the inclusion of kicking and elbowing techniques, Marquis of Queensberry rules are loosely observed.

Some modern writers have been wont to observe close similarities between the Medieval European knight and the samurai warriors of Japan. This comparison, though valid on the surface, cannot be carried too far since the samurai were equally at ease fighting on the ground as from horseback, whereas their heavily armored European counterparts were often like the proverbial "fish out of water" when unhorsed. What combat the steel-encased knights could participate in after the disaster of unhorsement generally involved the rather clumsy wielding of a heavy broadsword, a battle-axe, or a mace.

This and other comparisons lead to the conclusion that Western military science concerns itself largely with complex weaponry, whereas individual technique and "spirit" probably best summarize the fighting style of the East. From the time English longbows and cannons felled the flower of French knighthood at Crecy in 1346 to the present use of intercontinental missiles and intricate guidance systems, Western man has been preoccupied with the materiel of war.

If "instant genocide," then, is the West's answer to the intensely individualized martial dedication of Asia, why has the West been so completely captivated by the difficult and arduous art of karate? The answer might well be simple. The fact that the West, and particularly the United States, has in recent years been exploring with great interest the more esoteric ideas and arts of the East was the natural result of the Allied occupation of Japan and Korea when ancient Asian cultures came under the sharp scrutiny of thousands of military and civilian personnel. Those who found their way off of Japan's glittering Ginza discovered a "new world" in the parts of this land where the people lived in the traditional manner. Many present-day "Asiaphiles" trace their interest in the Orient back to such post-World War II military duty in Japan or Korea.

The Effect of Asian Immigration

Also to be considered is the fact that, in California at

least, groundwork for the entry of these arts into the United States had been laid decades before. Chinese, Japanese, and Okinawans had been immigrating sporadically since the turn of the century, and they quite naturally brought their cultures with them. It is well known that the practice of *ch'uan fa* and karate was common within these ethnic groups.

More specifically, the late nineteenth century was a period of rather extensive Chinese labor migrations to the Hawaiian Islands and the western United States. The gold fever in California and the subsequent railroad building boom were jointly responsible for the importation of thousands of indentured Chinese citizens by wealthy speculators and Chinese business groups. This labor community in California was first welcomed; but as organized labor saw the great competition offered by these contract workers from across the Pacific, a cloud of prejudice formed that soon enveloped the whole of "Chinese California." This fear of cheap Chinese labor was the cause of the so-called "Yellow Peril," an idea based on economic considerations and fanciful ideas of mass Oriental migrations and their ultimate control of the entire West Coast. This prejudice was instrumental in halting Chinese immigration to the United States and her possessions, in the passage of a series of exclusionary laws beginning with the Chinese Exclusion Act of 1882,[1] and ending with total exclusion of Chinese laborers in 1904.[2] However, this legislation came too late to prevent the seed of Chinese culture from being planted in American soil.

Few of the immigrant Chinese adopted an Americanized way of living, since their primary interest was in fulfilling their contractual agreements with the Chinese or American hiring agent. As it turned out, however, most of the indentured workers stayed on in the United States. They constructed virtually self-contained communities called

"Chinatowns"—a term first mentioned in California newspapers in 1853[3]—and lived much as they did in their native country.

It is only now becoming apparent that the intricate web of Chinese society in California was never fully understood. Chinese sojourners coming to the United States in search of the promised quick wealth brought with them all the prejudices, fears, and rivalries that had existed in their homeland. A series of district companies based on ties with China-based companies, along with fraternal associations based on surname or place of origin in China, governed the Chinese sojourners' lives so completely that in many instances they were little more than slaves. Merchant companies, called *kongsi,* were formed and headed by members of the Chinese merchant class.[4] At the same time secret societies (*hui*) existed that controlled massive groups of Chinese laborers by the threat of death. Behind a facade of benevolence these organizations, in the 1850s and later, oppressed their countrymen to the point where incidents of violence became common between various Chinese groups.[5] Coupled with the fact that rival factions fought bitterly for supremacy in certain spheres of commerce (e.g., gambling and prostitution rights to labor camps) it is small wonder that Chinatowns in the West saw blood purges on a regular basis. In one of the most notable feuds, the *Hung Shun T'ang,* which controlled San Francisco's Chinatown, clashed with the *I Hing T'ang,* a group controlling the mining districts' Chinese laborers. Traditional feuds were also carried on, such as those between Hakka and Punti Chinese, and the more frequent battles between *kongsi* factions representing their counterparts in Canton and Hong Kong.[6] Blacksmiths in Trinity County, California, were hired to make the traditional Chinese weapons of war such as tridents, spears, pike poles, brush scythes, and bamboo shields.[7] Some rival companies even held public drills and parades in the mining town streets.[8] Amused non-Chinese workers lined the perimeter of the battles to cheer and to bet on their favorites, and some went so far as to serve as mercenaries with one or more of the rival factions.

Americans in the western United States, and particularly California, came to know of these battles as "tong wars," because in the United States the Chinese secret societies were called "tongs," which is the Cantonese pronunciation of the ideograph 堂 *t'ang,* meaning "hall" or "office."[9] The most notorious *t'ang* "enforcers" were called "hatchet men" (*boo tow doy*) because of the meat cleaver that they so skillfully wielded when dispatching opponents. Most of these "hatchet men" were also skilled in the *ch'uan fa* fighting techniques and other intricate arts such as pin-blowing and coin-flipping. Pin-blowing is an art common to several Asian countries, but most notably China and Japan. The technique is simple. An expert carries a number of sharpened pins in his mouth and blows one out at a time with a quick exhaling action. Ninja in feudal Japan are said to have perfected pin-blowing to an amazing degree of accuracy up to a twenty-foot distance.

Coin-flipping consists of throwing, or flipping with the thumb, a coin whose edges have been honed to razor sharpness. The primary targets are the jugular vein and the eye. Proponents of this art can stand, arms folded, and with a simple motion imbed a heavy coin half its width into a hardwood backstop. (This fact can be attested to, the author having seen such a demonstration in Honolulu in 1961.)

In 1898 San Francisco police Lieutenant William Price estimated that of the less than three thousand "highbinders" (the term given these "hatchet men" in California) in San Francisco, between three hundred and five hundred earned some part of their living by killing for hire.[10]

An interesting feature of the many California *t'angs* was their close affiliation with the Triad Lodges in China and Southeast Asia.[11] The Chinese Triad Society was a seventeenth-century organization formed for the specific purpose of subverting the controlling power in China at that time, the Manchu Ch'ing dynasty. When this group was broken up by Manchu forces in the eighteenth century, five Buddhist monks secretly reorganized the Five Provincial Grand Lodges of the Triad Society, and continued working secretly to overthrow the Manchus.[12] Tradition states that these five monks were *ch'uan fa* masters and that for many years they instructed masses of people in the use of the art as an offensive tactic against the Manchu soldiers.

A police raid on a secret society in San Francisco in 1853 showed that the group was an American arm of a Chinese-based Triad group. At that time the combined Triad forces controlled the walled city of Shanghai by force of arms, and were largely dependent on financial assistance from their brethren on this side of the Pacific.[13] The American Triad societies exacted heavy conscriptions from their members—whether willing or not—in sums as high as $150,000 a year,[14] and made further profits by conducting illicit businesses such as gambling, prostitution, and trafficking in opium.[15]

As the Chinese in the western United States became increasingly better accepted by American society, their role as menial laborers underwent a marked change. They worked predominantly as farmers, merchants, laundry owners, and cafe proprietors, and many chose to sever their ties with China and take American citizenship. This, combined with the crackdown on vice in Chinatowns throughout California, helped put an end to the *t'ang's* iron grip on the Chinese-American community, so that by 1930 the Triad Society was under police control and surveillance, but by no means defunct.

Ch'uan fa, used offensively at the height of the *t'ang* crisis, once again became an exercise ritual and holiday spectacle for the Chinese community. Most Chinese-American societies sponsored *ch'uan fa* practices, limiting participation to those of immediate Chinese ancestry. The slow opening of *ch'uan fa* to non-Chinese practitioners did not come until two decades after World War II.

With *t'ang* warfare and intense racial discrimination headlining the hardships of the Chinese in California, many Chinese emigrants chose to disembark in the then-Kingdom of Hawaii. They generally fared much better in their relations with each other and with their non-Chinese bosses. Organizations similar to the *t'ang* and *hui* groups of western America were founded in Hawaii, and by 1889 the first Chinese society—the Ket On Association—was born.[16] As the Chinese had no consular representatives in the Hawaiian Islands (then a monarchy ruled by Queen Liliuokalani), it became the Ket On Association's function to aid members of the Chinese community in legal matters and in "benevolent practices" (e.g., obtaining burial funds for indigent Chinese, etc.).[17] Most of the Chinese societies that formed after the Ket On Association were exclusive, in that they limited membership to those whose ancestry could be traced to a specific Chinese district or province.[18]

It has been previously noted that overseas Chinese communities have typically been isolated, introverted, and highly exclusive as regards their ethnic arts and crafts. Since earliest recorded history, the Chinese have maintained extreme pride in their indigenous arts and have guarded their public exhibition and knowledge very closely. Thus it is understandable that these societies continued to be restrictive on the basis of surname or location of ancestry in China, and that an art like *ch'uan fa,* which was very restrictive in China, would remain so in Hawaii. To some extent, *ch'uan fa* was practiced within the confines of these societies as a type of physical exercise, like calisthenics. These exercise sessions, though not officially sponsored by the various societies, were generally conducted by members who had achieved recognition for their *ch'uan fa* skills in the Chinese province from which they came.

In 1922 the Chinese Physical Culture Association was founded in Honolulu, Hawaii. Its purpose was to promote physical culture among the islands' Chinese communities.[19] This club was the first organization to practice *ch'uan fa* (known in Hawaii by the popular term "kung fu") in organized classes with several instructors from different Chinese provinces.[20] This association remains alive and very active to this day.

Non-Chinese were able to gain fleeting glimpses of *ch'uan fa* techniques both in Hawaii and most of California during the Chinese New Year celebration held in February. This is the most lavishly celebrated of the Chinese holy days, and there are records of the famous dragon dances and fireworks displays taking place in California as early as the 1850s.[21] The dragon and lion dances are highlights of the New Year, and are the major source of attraction for tourists visiting the various Chinatowns. Almost unnoticed, and very rarely understood when observed, are the accompanying *ch'uan fa* acrobatics generally performed by the young Chinese representatives of the *ch'uan fa* clubs. Though never lacking in enthusiasm, these boys are rarely adept at the art of *ch'uan fa* and thus attract less attention to the art than would highly skillful exponents.

This, it seems, is done purposely by the heads of the organizational hierarchy of the Chinese societies. However, according to a spokesman of the United Chinese Society—the 110-year old "parent" organization for all Chinese societies in the Hawaiian Islands—*ch'uan fa* has not purposely been kept from the non-Chinese, nor are there any written rules that specifically exclude non-Chinese from participating in *ch'uan fa* associations.[22] But it is evident that, notwithstanding the absence of a clearly documented policy, there has long been an unwritten law prohibiting non-Chinese from participating in the numerous Chinese societies' activities. (The author in fact attempted to secure *ch'uan fa* instruction in 1958 at the Chinese Physical Culture Association in Honolulu, and was refused admission. Although other reasons were given, it was evident that the real reason for rejection was non-Chinese ancestry.) It can be concluded that in practice, *ch'uan fa* had been restrictive on the basis of national origin in the Hawaiian Islands as well as elsewhere until 1957.

Mr. Tinn Chan Lee, a master of t'ai chi ch'uan, was the first Chinese martial arts instructor known to have opened his teachings to the general public. Mr. Lee began t'ai chi classes at the Mun Lum School (Chinese language school) in Honolulu in 1957.[23] Since that initial public class, Mr. Lee has instructed various clubs and organizations, and given lecture-demonstrations to numbers of Asian study groups.

Since Mr. Lee is a naturalized citizen from China, his background is quite interesting. He first came to Hawaii in 1923 where he worked in the electronics field. In 1937 he returned to China to renew his *ch'uan fa* training, which had begun when he was very young. His instructor was one of the two great living proponents of t'ai chi ch'uan, Master Kam Chin Wu.[24] After receiving an advanced degree, he returned to Honolulu and soon thereafter opened the electrical repair and appliance store that he operated into the 1960s.

When dealing with a person with as interesting a personal history as Mr. Lee's, one is very likely to wonder why a naturalized Chinese-American instead of a second- or third-generation Chinese-American would be the first to break the traditional barrier of *ch'uan fa* secrecy. The first of two possible explanations is that the art of t'ai chi ch'uan is one of the less apparently "lethal" forms of *ch'uan fa,* though in the hands of experts, t'ai chi is certainly an effective fighting art. In the documentary film *Beyond the Great Wall,* t'ai chi practices were shown. In certain parts of the film elderly men could be seen performing the graceful movements of *ch'uan fa.* In fact, Mr. Lee's stated premise for including non-Chinese in his t'ai chi classes was based on the physical culture aspect of such teaching.[25] The second reason may be that Lee felt a patriotic duty toward the United States, and wanted to express his thanks for the hospitality he had received and for the benefits of being a citizen of his adopted country.[26] This type of loyalty, as we shall see later in the chapter, has not been uncommon among naturalized Americans of Asian ancestry.

Development in Hawaii Before World War II

Modern Hawaii has been called the "melting pot" of the world due to the large-scale intermarriage of members of its ethnic communities. In breaking the population into ethnic groups we see that the Japanese constitute nearly one-third of the islands' total population (which traditionally includes those of Okinawan ancestry). The Chinese make up the next largest Oriental segment, followed by members of the Korean-American community.[27]

The great bulk of Okinawan emigrants came to Hawaii between 1880–1910.[28] As Okinawa was then politically a part of the Japanese Empire, these people were classified as Japanese in the various census polls. In 1924 the Japanese Consulate General for Hawaii listed the Okinawan population as 16,536 or 13.8 % of the total Japanese population.[29] If there has been no great difference in rate of population growth between Okinawans and non-Okinawan-Japanese since that time, we can estimate that in 1950 there were about twenty-six thousand people of direct Okinawan ancestry living on all of the islands of Hawaii.

Following the United States' nineteenth-century policy of excluding further Chinese labor immigrations, the Hawaiian legislature in 1887 and 1888 enacted similar laws to stop the flow of Chinese field workers.[30] The American planters living in the Hawaiian Islands then turned to Japan as their next source of cheap labor. Although a small scattering of Japanese emigrants had come to Hawaii as early as 1868,[31] their greatest numbers arrived between 1885 and 1894—nearly thirty thousand in all.[32] By 1900 Hawaii had over sixty-one thousand Japanese, or about forty percent of the total population.[33]

The Hawaiian government, alarmed by the explosion of the Japanese population, finally refused further admission of Japanese contract workers, and returned to Japan over a thousand recently arrived laborers.[34] Japanese diplomats regarded this nonadmission policy as an insult, and sent a warship along with a demand for indemnification.

Upon tacit approval of the United States, which was then in the process of annexing these islands, Hawaii paid an indemnity of seventy-five thousand dollars, after which Japan withdrew her complaint.[35]

Shortly thereafter, Japanese immigration to US possessions was hindered by the so-called "Gentlemen's Agreement" that stopped the labor migrations in exchange for an American commitment promising no open discrimination against the Japanese already in the country.[36] Two decades later, Congress passed the "Japanese Exclusion Act,"[37] which arose out of anti-Japanese feelings that had been developing in California. This antagonism had evolved from a rather vaguely stated concept that the Japanese constituted a threat to the security of California because of their general adherence to the cultural patterns of their homeland. It has been argued, however, that the primary fear was of the agricultural prowess of the Japanese family farms, which were producing more cash crops per acre than their Caucasian counterparts. Had it not been for President Theodore Roosevelt's firm stand for fairer treatment of the Japanese on the West Coast, these people would undoubtedly have experienced even more intensely prejudicial treatment than they did.[38] After 1924, immigration from Japan and Okinawa virtually ceased, except for small numbers of teachers, students, "picture brides," priests, *kibei* (those born in the United States, but sent to Japan for their education), and persons with temporary visas.

As Chinese *ch'uan fa* had come with the earliest Chinese sojourners to the mainland United States and the Hawaiian Islands, so did karate enter with Okinawan immigrants. Most Okinawans who emigrated to Hawaii and California prior to 1903 generally lacked training in this art due to its secrecy and selectivity. However, there was at least one Okinawan immigrant in Honolulu who had begun his karate training at the age of nine in 1894 in Naha and had continued for eleven years before coming to Hawaii in 1905.[39] From 1903 onward those with an educational background knew at least the fundamental basics of karate, since, beginning in that year, karate became a standard part of the Okinawan schools' physical education program. In fact, every boy who reached the intermediate grades received karate instruction. As a result, the number of karate practitioners among Okinawan immigrants in Hawaii and California is virtually impossible to gauge.

Undoubtedly many Okinawans had been practicing the art throughout most of their lives. Few, however, advertised knowledge of their karate skills or undertook to teach others their art. The reason for this seems to have been the traditional secrecy that karate underwent after Satsuma's invasion of the Ryukyus in 1609, and the fact that during the early days after Japan's formal annexation of these islands in 1875 the various karate schools of Naha, Shuri, and Tomari engaged each other in competitions that amounted to combat. Okinawan emigrants from these villages carried the old hostilities with them to their new homes in the West. Very few wanted to openly teach karate for fear that a rival would learn their secrets. Thus, karate remained more of a family art than something that was available to all of the Okinawan community.

It is also true that most of the Okinawan sojourners lacked sufficient training in karate to instruct others in the art. A majority of the karate students simply practiced the various *kata* movements in the privacy of their homes. It was not until 1927 that the first recognized master of karate entered the Hawaiian Islands.

Kensu Yabu, one of the early Okinawan karate masters and a retired lieutenant of the Japanese Army, introduced his form of the art to Hawaii in 1927. While returning from a personal business trip to the mainland United States, Yabu was persuaded by a group of Okinawan citizens to stop in the islands for a short while for the purpose of teaching karate. Yabu consented to do so, and taught karate in the private homes of a number of Okinawans.[40] In April, 1927, he presented the first public karate demonstration at the Nuuanu YMCA in Honolulu, and although the demonstration was open to the public, nearly all of the spectators were Okinawans.[41]

Kensu Yabu traveled to the island of Kauai, Territory of Hawaii, in the latter part of April giving lectures and karate demonstrations at a number of towns.[42] After approximately five months of teaching karate in the Hawaiian Islands, Master Yabu returned to his home on Okinawa.

The ramifications of Yabu's short visit to Hawaii were manifold. First, non-Okinawans witnessed for the first time a karate performance by a recognized authority. The few *naichi* Japanese (i.e., Japanese from one of the four main islands of Japan) who observed Yabu's YMCA demonstration saw karate to be a strong fighting art, possibly even stronger than their judo. This interest in karate by non-Okinawans thereafter ebbed and flowed until the post-World War II period. Yabu's arrival solidified the Okinawan karate enthusiasts in Hawaii who had previously studied only in the seclusion of their homes. His open teachings brought interested groups of Okinawans together for practice and recreation, something the rivalries of Naha, Shuri, and Tomari had prevented on Okinawa.

The Hawaii of the late 1920s and early 1930s saw promoters matching judoists against boxers. Since such contests were publicly acclaimed and highly profitable, a group of Okinawan men decided to combine their resources and bring from Okinawa a karate expert to pit against some of the well-known island fighters.[43] This promotional group selected the famous Choki Motobu as their karate champion.

Motobu's history reads much like a Hemingway characterization. He was reputed to have defeated Russia's heavyweight boxing champion in a bare-handed contest in 1924.[44] Although documentation for this bout is lacking, Motobu's reputation as a strongman and fighter is legendary among contemporary Okinawan and Japanese peoples. Complications arose, however, over Motobu's visa and he was not permitted to remain in Hawaii after arriving at the Immigration Station in 1932.[45] The United States Immigration Office does not release classified information concerning immigrants, and so their refusal to grant Motobu a temporary visa will never be completely understood. On the other hand, speculation centers around Motobu's record as a brawler, that, in their opinion, served to brand him as an undesirable.

Undaunted by this initial failure in promoting karate

versus boxing, the aforementioned Okinawan group attempted to bring to Hawaii other karate experts for this purpose. Their second selection was two Okinawan students of high moral caliber, both of whom had studied at leading Japanese universities. They were Zuiho Mutsu and Kamesuke Higaonna.

Mutsu and Higaonna came to Hawaii in 1933 with the understanding that they would be teaching and lecturing on the art of karate, not exhibiting their art in the boxing ring.[46] Both flatly refused to engage in the proposed matches on the grounds that karate was too dangerous for such contests.[47] Thomas Miyashiro, son of an Okinawan immigrant, had studied with Yabu in 1927, and was thus a highly respected member of the Okinawan community in Hawaii. He convinced most of the Okinawan karate enthusiasts to approach Mutsu and Higaonna en masse and request that they remain in Hawaii to teach karate publicly.[48] The two Okinawan *sensei* agreed, and soon thereafter opened a school at the Asahi Photo Studio near Honolulu's Aala Park.[49] Miyashiro joined the teaching staff as assistant instructor and interpreter, and soon the school was filled with Okinawan-American and Japanese-American students. Because of the rapidity with which the school grew, larger quarters were soon needed. The new site chosen was the Izumo Taisha Shinto Mission near the intersection of King and Beretania Streets, also in Honolulu.

A club was formed from these classes, called the Hawaii Karate Seinin Kai (Hawaii Young People's Karate Club).[50] Shortly thereafter this group staged a public demonstration at the Honolulu Civic Auditorium.[51] A number of Caucasian spectators viewing this display became interested in learning karate. Most of these young men were members of the First Methodist Church located on Beretania Street, next to the Honolulu Academy of Arts. Through their efforts, in 1933 the first known Caucasian group in the Western world to openly study and sponsor karate activities was formed.[52]

The three instructors of the Hawaii Karate Seinin Kai presided over each karate practice held several nights a week in the church basement. The most remarkable thing about this development is the fact that at that time the rapport that is presently enjoyed between Asian and non-Asian peoples did not exist. In fact, these young Caucasians and all others who studied Oriental arts in the pre-World War II period were considered very eccentric and were highly criticized by certain segments of the Caucasian community.

A Lieutenant Moore of the Army Air Corps, coach of the Wheeler Air Field's boxing and wrestling teams, was a member of this church group's karate class. His efforts and interest in karate, coupled with help from Mr. Miyashiro, brought visiting Okinawan karate instructors and students to Wheeler Air Field to give karate instruction.[53] It is very likely that the American military's first contact with karate occurred at this time, a scant eighteen years after the art's formal introduction into Japan by Gichin Funakoshi. Late in 1933 Mutsu returned to Japan to resume his duties as vice-president of Imperial University's (presently the University of Tokyo) Karate Study Club.[54] Higaonna returned to Japan shortly thereafter at which time Mr. Miyashiro assumed leadership of the Hawaii Karate Seinin Kai. He elected to continue classes at the Izumo Taisha Mission, First Methodist Church, and Wheeler Field, and to open several new locations in rural Oahu.

Until now karate had remained a very esoteric art. Though most Japanese- and Okinawan-American participants understood that there was a fundamental philosophy underlying karate practice, few others were aware that there was any more to it than the physical defense techniques.

Due primarily to the Okinawan community's interest in

furthering karate practice in Hawaii, Mr. Chinei Kinjo, editor of the Okinawan newspaper *Yoen Jiho Sha* published on the island of Kauai, invited the famous Okinawan karate master Chojun Miyagi to come to Hawaii in 1934 to teach karate.[55] Co-sponsors of Miyagi's trip were the Lihue Young Buddhist Association's Judo Club and the Okinawa Kenjin Kai (Okinawa Prefectural People's Club).[56]

For the Hawaiian Islands to receive such a renowned master of karate was indeed a fortunate occurrence. His impact on the local scene can best be gleaned from a translation of the *Yoen Jiho Sha's* article of May 1, 1934:

> Long awaited Mr. Miyagi finally arrives . . .
> Chojun Miyagi, the recognized authority of Ryukyu karate and master of unmeasurable skill, was prepared to visit Hawaii on invitation of this company. But due to various difficulties his departure from Okinawa has been postponed many times. Anxious karate fans of the Hawaiian Islands began sending inquiries as to the exact date of his arrival . . . We were relieved to hear from Mr. Miyagi by telegram, on the twenty-sixth, "Am leaving today."
> Many requests have been received from various islands to the effect that in the event of his arrival he ought to visit that island first, but upon his arrival, after one or two demonstrations in Honolulu first, we will ask him to go completely around this island (Kauai). We are considering asking him to visit other islands afterward. Soon after the announcement of the forthcoming visit of Mr. Chojun Miyagi, we were approached by policemen . . . of Waimea expressing the desire of the police department for him to give demonstrations for the policemen of this island. Since we acknowledge their request gladly, we will consult Mr. Miyagi when he arrives and it seems that the exhibition will take

place in the presence of all the policemen of this island.

Concerning the visit, well-wishers of the various islands had tremendous expectation and many pledged their support . . .

As already reported, Mr. Miyagi is the master of karate at Taiiku Kyokai (Health Institute) operated by the Government of Okinawa and as far as his profound knowledge in his art is concerned, no one in all of Okinawa Prefecture can equal him. In Okinawa he participates wherever karate is practiced. Prior to his departure to Hawaii, he conducted a one-week seminar . . . sponsored by the Okinawa Branch of the Dai Nippon Butokukai. Studying until October 1915 under the supervision of the late Kanryo Higaonna, renowned master of Chinese *kempo* (*ch'uan fa*), he sought profound knowledge. Twice he went to . . . China, once in May of 1915 and . . . in July of 1917, and studied and made research on the Chinese art . . . In 1926 he planned to improve and unify karate. In order to carry out his plan he rallied his companions and established the Okinawa Karate-jutsu Kenkyu Kai (Okinawa Karate Research Club) . . . In 1926, he accepted a part-time professorship at the First Budo Seminar under the auspices of the Dai Nippon Butokukai Okinawa Committee. He was invited to be karate instructor in the Judo Department of Kyoto University in October 1928 . . . In June 1932, he was invited by the Karate Department of Kansai University in Osaka, where he coached karate. In May 1932, he visited Tokyo. By earnest request of karate and boxing clubs of various schools in the city, he conducted lectures and gave demonstrations . . . [57]

Miyagi's arrival in Hawaii created quite a stir among the

islands' martial arts devotees. He toured a number of towns in rural Oahu and Honolulu to answer their requests for karate demonstrations. The popularity of the Okinawan master was such that great numbers of Caucasians came to observe his karate lecture-demonstrations, and they moved one newspaper reporter to remark "this is true karate."[58] In the latter part of May, 1934, Miyagi traveled to the island of Kauai where he performed in Waimea, Hanalei, Koloa, and Hanapepe, and gave a series of special demonstrations to the island's police force.

On May 29, 1934, an article in the *Yoen Jiho Sha* advertised that students wishing to learn *kempo-karate* should apply immediately for such instruction. The term "kempo-karate" should be remembered because future instructors in these arts used this combination in the post-World War II period. "Kempo" is simply the Japanese way of pronouncing the Chinese ideographs representing the word "ch'uan fa." Miyagi continued his teaching on Kauai until January 15, 1935, at which time he returned to Okinawa where business matters demanded his personal attention.[59] His sojourn in Hawaii lasted approximately eight months, during which time he directly assisted over a hundred karate students.

Except for Thomas Miyashiro's karate classes in Professor Henry Okazaki's judo gymnasium, which continued to 1936,[60] Miyagi's return to Okinawa in 1935 virtually ended the short but dynamic period of karate establishment and growth in Hawaii. From then to 1942 a period of quiet prevailed in Hawaiian karate circles. The Hawaii Karate Seinin Kai ceased to exist after Mr. Miyashiro's retirement and for several years following 1936 there were no known karate instructors openly teaching the art. As in the pre-1927 era, karate practice returned to the Okinawan community where small groups continued in semiprivate. The great interest in karate fostered by Yabu, Mutsu, Higaonna,

Miyagi, and Miyashiro, would not be rekindled until a Hawaiian-born Japanese-American named James M. Mitose entered the martial arts scene at the outbreak of World War II.

Virtually all of the Hawaiian-born karate enthusiasts felt that karate was a post-World War II phenomenon. This misassumption is based both on the lack of knowledge of the 1927–1936 era and the fact that Dr. Mitose's style was not karate at all, but was the remote ancestor, *Shorinji kempo* (the Japanese way of pronouncing *Shaolin ch'uan fa*). It was not until after the Korean conflict that karate per se made its reappearance.

Dr. Mitose was born in Hawaii in 1916. At age five he was sent to Kyushu, Japan, for schooling in his ancestor's art of self-defense called *Kosho-ryu kempo.* From 1921 to 1936 he studied and mastered this art, which is based directly on Bodhidharma's *Shaolin ch'uan fa.*[61] The Mitose family tradition states that members of their clan in Kumamoto and Nagasaki brought the knowledge of *Shaolin ch'uan fa* from China shortly before the Tokugawa period, which began in 1615. This art was modified through the years by successive Mitose *kempo* masters until the *Kosho-ryu,* or "Old Pine Tree Style," *kempo* was born.[62] Mitose's *kempo* is not Okinawan karate, a fact made abundantly clear by Mitose's explanation of the many facets of *kempo* that do not involve combative techniques. However, some of the *kata* forms of the *Kosho-ryu* resemble, and in a few instances are duplicated in, certain styles of karate. This is certainly to be expected when one realizes how heavily Okinawan karate borrowed from Chinese *ch'uan fa.* An example of similarity between *Kosho-ryu kempo* and Okinawan karate is found in the *kata* called *Naihanchi.* Dr. Mitose explains that the philosophical significance of this *kata,* seldom if ever acknowledged in karate, is always explained to a student of *Kosho-ryu kempo* before the physical combat form is taught.[63]

Kosho-ryu kempo is truly a remarkable art. In essence, the ideals of Zen Buddhism as expounded by Bodhidharma and the great Zen master and patriarch Rinzai (Lin-chih), are fundamental to the physical manifestations of the *Kosho-ryu* fighting art. The development of restraint, propriety, humbleness, and integrity, therefore, are the cornerstones of *Kosho-ryu kempo,* and the actual combat techniques merely one of the many modes of reaching these goals. *Kempo* training in its entirety consists of intensive instruction in Buddhist philosophy, general education, the human body and its systems, as well as training in kendo (fencing), *kyudo* (archery), *ikebana* (flower arranging), swimming, tree-climbing, horsemanship, use of the blowgun, and the weaponless forms of traditional *Shaolin ch'uan fa.*[64]

Kosho-ryu kempo, therefore, is more than just another style of unarmed self-defense; it is a way of life complete with a socially significant philosophy that is capsulized in the term "self-defense." Only in the most extreme instances of life-threatening aggression are the fighting arts brought into play; and even then they are designed to bring the opponent to the awareness of his wrong rather than to maim or injure him.

After completing his training in Japan, Dr. Mitose returned to Hawaii in 1936.[65] The final incidents leading up to World War II, contrasted with America's previously quasi-cordial involvement with the Japanese Empire, placed Dr. Mitose in the complex role of dual loyalties, as was the case of all *kibei.* Mitose explains his feelings at that time:

> My position was different from that of most Americans. I had lived happily in America as an American citizen. I loved America and its institutions and felt it was my duty to take up arms for this country whose privileges had been generously extended to me. On the other hand it was not as simple a decision as it

> would be for most. I had spent the formative years of my life in Japan, and had some relatives still living in Japan to whom I was bound by every tie of blood and experiences shared in common.[66]

On December 8, 1941, less than twenty-four hours after Japan's successful strike against the United States Naval Base at Pearl Harbor, James Mitose made his decision and entered the Hawaii Territorial Guard.[67] Feeling that his *kempo* art should then be shared with the country of his birth, Territory of Hawaii, U.S.A., Dr. Mitose, in 1942, organized the Official Self-Defense Club at the Beretania Mission in Honolulu for the purpose of teaching " . . . the true meaning of self-defense."[68] This organization lasted until 1953 under the leadership of Mitose,[69] and later was in the hands of one of his disciples, Thomas Young.

Because of Dr. Mitose's intense dedication to the *kempo* "way of life," he was somewhat of an enigma to the sports-minded people of Hawaii, as well as to many who studied with him. When the doors of the Official Self-Defense Club opened for the first time, the majority of aspirants to respond were non-Okinawan, non-Japanese. It seemed inevitable that these people would be unable to fully comprehend—much less to live up to—the total life involvement required by the study of *Kosho-ryu kempo,* and that most of them would not want Asian morality mixed in with their martial arts training. The fundamental disparity that then arose between master and pupils naturally limited the number of students that would choose to pursue *kempo* studies. Thus, at the time of Mitose's departure for the United States mainland in 1953, only five pupils—Thomas Young, William Chow, Paul Yamaguchi, Arthur Keawe, and Edward Lowe—had attained the *shodan* or first-degree black belt.[70]

After ten years of attempting to teach the gamut of skills

that comprised *Kosho-ryu kempo,* Dr. Mitose wrote a book entitled *What Is Self-Defense?* In it he explained his position and philosophy in regard to self-defense study; but at the insistence of the publisher, the book included hundreds of photos of self-defense techniques. Thus the average reader is led to believe that, indeed, this is merely another empty-handed martial art. Shortly thereafter, Dr. Mitose retired from active *kempo* instruction and left the Hawaiian Islands for the United States, there to pursue the studies that ultimately led to his ordination as a Christian minister, and the attainment of the doctors of theology and philosophy degrees.

Kempo arts did not expire after Dr. Mitose left the Hawaiian Islands; rather, an increased interest in unarmed combat grew due to the teachings of the Mitose graduates. Three of his *shodan* grantees formed clubs of their own, while the fourth, Thomas Young, assumed control of the Official Self-Defense Club.

Thomas Young, a soft-spoken and intelligent Chinese-American, probably best epitomized the type of individual Mitose was looking for when he began *kempo* instruction in 1942. Young was a student of *ch'uan fa* in his youth and his interest in these arts led him to seek out Mitose when he learned of *Kosho-ryu kempo.* He began his training in this art primarily because of deep involvement with the principles of self-defense as expounded in Dr. Mitose's *Kosho-ryu kempo* philosophy.[71] As of 1966, Mr. Young had graduated a number of *shodan,* including some who have gone on to form *kempo* clubs in Hawaii and on the mainland United States.[72]

Two other former Mitose pupils were standouts in the Hawaiian martial arts scene. They are William Chow and Edward "Bobby" Lowe. Chow received his *shodan* in 1946, and three years later formed his own club at the Nuuanu YMCA.[73] The unusual aspect of this organization was the fact that it was called a "kempo-karate" school. As Mitose had never associated *Kosho-ryu kempo* with Okinawan karate in any manner, it is difficult to understand this move by Chow. "Kempo-karate," was first used in 1934 when the *Yoen Jiho Sha* newspaper advertised for prospective students for Chojun Miyagi's Hawaiian visit. And, since Miyagi was well aware that *kempo* and *ch'uan fa* were synonymous, his choice of the term probably meant that his style of karate (*Goju-ryu)* was a combination of Chinese *ch'uan fa* and Okinawan karate. Perhaps Chow's use of the word "karate," which was far better known in Hawaii than "kempo," was simply his way of attracting more students to his school. But however that may be, William Chow has trained and awarded the *shodan* to a large number of students since 1949, all of whom claim mastery in this nebulous art of "kempo-karate." Edward Lowe's significance will be discussed in conjunction with the post-Korean War karate development.

Post–Korean War Development in Hawaii

The re-entry of "pure" or Okinawan karate to the active Hawaiian martial arts picture occurred in 1956, though the roots had taken hold after World War II when many servicemen were stationed in Japan. Many Hawaiian-born second- (*nisei)* and third-generation (*sansei)* Japanese-Americans found occupation duty in their ancestral homeland an enlightening experience. Most of them, having been reared in contact with grandparents whose memories of Japan were still fresh, had a "feeling" for these arts that by then had been identified with Japanese culture, and so many took up the study of karate, some even studying with the great names of Japanese karate. These *nisei* and *sansei* were shortly to become the "new breed," as it were, of American karate.

Such, for example, was Carlton Shimomi. By organizing

the *Shorin-ryu* karate club in Kapahulu (Honolulu), in August of 1956, he became the first to reintroduce "pure" karate into the Hawaiian Islands.[74] Shimomi had studied *Shorin-ryu* karate in Fukuoka, Japan, while a member of the armed forces. This style, founded in the Ryukyu Islands, was brought to Japan after 1915 and grew in popularity until it became one of the styles that is practiced in Japanese universities today.

Walter Nishioka, another *Shorin-ryu* expert, followed quickly in Carlton Shimomi's footsteps by organizing the Goshinkai Karate School in July of 1957. Nishioka received his *shodan* in Japan, and had studied for a length of time on Okinawa as well.[75]

Chojun Miyagi's *Goju-ryu* karate was reactivated in the Hawaiian Islands by Mitsugi Kobayashi, George Miyasaki, and Kenneth Murakami. The latter two, while in the Air Force, studied in Kawasaki City, Japan, with one of the few existing *ju-dan* (tenth degree), Professor Kanki Izumikawa. Upon returning to Hawaii they established the Senbukan, Hawaii Branch, *Goju-ryu* Karate School. Kobayashi received his training from the famous Master Higa of Okinawa while working for the United States Civil Service,[76] and opened the Kobayashi *Dojo* in Hawaii after completing his service on Okinawa.

Since Okinawan karate's reintroduction into Hawaii by Carlton Shimomi in 1956, there has been a steady increase in the number of competing schools, or styles (*ryu*). Although many of these styles are orthodox karate forms, it has become an all-too-common practice for an individual to earn the *shodan* in two or more *ryu* and then to teach what he feels are the best techniques of each. The results are quite evident. For example, of the five Mitose graduates only Thomas Young stayed with the *kempo* style of his teacher. Edward "Bobby" Lowe probably deviated from *Kosho-ryu kempo* the most markedly, since in 1958 he affiliated his school of self-defense with Masatatsu Oyama's Kyokushinkai of Tokyo. Oyama's style is known for its lethality and for the violence that it has been wont to display. In fact, Oyama gained notoriety by touring various areas of the world and killing a number of full-grown bulls with his bare hands under controlled conditions. His compact with Mr. Lowe is stated in the following letter:

> The Hawaii Kyokushinkai is affiliated with the Tokyo Kyokushinkai and was designated on 15 November, 1958 as the bona-fide representative in Honolulu of the Nippon Karate-do Kyokushinkai and is fully qualified to use . . . styles of Oyama dojo.[77]

This type of affiliation is still being carried on today. Other graduates of the "Mitose line" have continually traveled to Japan for further training and it seems likely that little of the original *Kosho-ryu kempo* will survive another decade of karate growth. In June, 1959, five men formed the Hawaii Karate Association. They were Paul Yamaguchi, a Mitose graduate; Carlton Shimomi of *Shorin-ryu;* and instructors Mitsugi Kobayashi, George Miyasaki, and Kenneth Murakami of *Goju-ryu.*[78]

By 1961 these same instructors, plus a number of newer faces, combined to form the Hawaii Karate Congress, which united nine clubs under its leadership. The purpose of this congress was to:

1. Aid in the establishment of an amiable relationship and unity among the membership.
2. Enhance the progress and advancement of karate through the study and guidance of the teachings of karate.
3. Propagate goodwill.
4. Aid in every way the advancement of the art of karate

> as a recognized sport, and to help develop a much higher degree of sportsmanship.[79]

A spokesman for this organization indicated that the congress was the first of its kind in the world to combine different *ryu* under one head.[80]

On November 5, 1961, the Hawaii Karate Congress sponsored a karate exhibition at the Honolulu Civic Auditorium featuring guest stars from Japan, including tenth *dan* Kanki Izumikawa, fifth *dan* Hidetaka Nishiyama of *Shotokan* karate, and fourth *dan* Hirokata Kanazawa, former All-Japan *Shotokan* Freestyle Champion. This array of Japanese stars dazzled the huge crowd at the Honolulu Civic, and was undoubtedly the single greatest motivation for increased karate activity since Chojun Miyagi's journey to the islands in 1934.

From 1959 to the present decade, karate has experienced a rapid growth in the Hawaiian Islands. Since becoming the fiftieth state in that year, Hawaii has continually evolved as one of several centers of Asian martial arts, even to the point where visiting Japanese karate teams have been beaten by island karateka. The importance of Hawaii's role in karate development is indisputable; a number of Hawaiian-trained teachers were to leave their mark on mainland US karate development.

On the Mainland USA

The chronological development of Asian martial arts per se on the mainland United States is somewhat clouded until the 1960s. Earlier *ch'uan fa* practice in the various Chinese communities was discussed at length and was seen to be exclusively the domain of the Chinese. However, this changed in 1963. Bruce Lee, of future television, film, and martial arts fame, opened a kung fu studio in Seattle, Washington, and the school was open to all races.[81]

In 1964, Master Wong Ark Yuey opened his Wah Que Chinese Kung Fu studio in the Old Chinatown section of Los Angeles. There were no racial restrictions for membership.[82]

The doors were open now for other kung fu clubs and schools to continue Bruce Lee and Master Wong's ending of the unwritten law of accepting only Chinese students. This, however, did not evolve without some confrontation.

After Bruce Lee moved to Oakland, California in 1964 and opened up his second kung fu school, he was challenged by some members of the San Francisco Chinese martial arts community.[83] They felt that Lee was giving away secrets of kung fu that might later be turned against Chinese people. Lee believed such notions were completely outmoded and that if whites were "out" to injure Chinese, there were plenty of other means available. "After all," Lee said, "they're bigger."[84]

The group of Chinese martial artists that arrived had a challenger, and a scroll written in Chinese challenging Lee to a duel.[85] In effect, had the challenger from the local Chinese kung fu community beaten Bruce Lee, then Lee would have had to stop teaching non-Chinese. In a fight that was more farce than lethal, Lee soundly defeated the "local" champion and did not have any more difficulty with the Chinese and his choice of who he taught.[86]

Karate, on the other hand, was virtually nonexistent in the United States prior to the mid-1950s. From 1964 to 1966, over one hundred Okinawan-Americans in California were interviewed and none admitted to personal knowledge of the art, though most had a cursory familiarity with the term and what it represented. Although no evidence could be found of any local ongoing instruction in karate among the ranks of these people, there were several reports of individuals engaging in the practice before World War II. These stories centered around a Mr. Hokama and a Mr. Aragaki who were located in the Delano area of northern California in the 1930s.[87] However, neither of them was supposed to have maintained karate classes, which leads us to the interesting fact that none of the people who have fostered California's karate "craze" claim Okinawan ancestry.

Why the lack of karate activity among California's Okinawans when they were the same type of immigrants who originated karate practice in Hawaii? The possible explanations are diverse.

The Okinawans interviewed may have been feigning ignorance of the subject so that they could maintain the traditional secrecy that formerly surrounded karate in the Ryukyus. But this supposition seems less likely when it is noted that no difficulty was experienced in communicating with the Okinawans who were responsible for karate's early beginnings in Hawaii. Since the Okinawan immigrants in the United States came from approximately the same areas of Okinawa, why would secrecy exist in California and not Hawaii? One possible answer is that Orientals as a whole were treated poorly in California from the mid-1800s on. Another factor is that Okinawan people, with the Japanese and Japanese-Americans, were put into the infamous "relocation" camps during World War II and when the author interviewed many of these people in the 1950s and 1960s there was still a smoldering resentment towards Caucasians in general. Some readers may be surprised to learn that the Japanese population of Hawaii, which made up nearly one-third of the island's total in 1941, were not interned except for about fifteen hundred "specialized" Japanese. According to Bryan Niiya of the Japanese-American Museum in Los Angeles, these "specialized" individuals included language instructors and *budoka.*

Thus, even in today's era of greater racial tolerance, Caucasians who delve into Asian martial arts, crafts, language, etc. are still treated with a degree of caution and perhaps even suspicion. Having studied Asian history and philosophy, and practiced karate and kendo for nearly thirty years, I believe I have at least a partial answer. Many Caucasians jump into karate or similar martial arts with great enthusiasm, or begin Asian language study, only to find that they are ankle deep in a sea of tremendous depth. Their interest wanes, and they become like the numerous other dilettantes who leave the art or sport. Certainly, at the commercial *dojo* cash is usually the only prerequisite for entry.

Aside from the above possibilities, there is the fact that California-bred Okinawans reside in scattered areas rather than in close-knit communities such as the Chinese were wont to form. The common tie of blood and ethnic practices was seemingly not enough to bring these scattered Okinawans together for participation in their endemic pastime. Suffice it to say that those Okinawans who did practice karate did so to the exclusion of all others, such that karate was virtually absent from the American mainland prior to 1953.

The United States Air Force, interested in Japanese martial arts since the close of World War II, in 1953 sponsored instruction for their personnel in judo and karate. Waseda, Keio, and Takushoku universities offered karate instructors for these special Air Force classes, and, later in that same year, Hidetaka Nishiyama led an Air Force-sponsored tour of American air bases in the United States.[88] This tour, though limited to military installations, was the first broad introduction of karate to the American public.

The opening date of the first United States-based karate school is still debated. With hundreds of thousands of military personnel traveling to and from Okinawa and

The late Robert Trias, American karate pioneer.

Japan between 1945 and the present, some karate-trained individuals undoubtedly began karate instruction in their own hometowns. But the first documented commercial karate school was opened in 1946 in Phoenix, Arizona by Robert Trias.[89] Trias studied with Tong Gee Hsiang in *Hsing*

I Ch'uan and was also a student of the Okinawan master Choki Motobu of *Shorei-ryu* karate.

The next in line was Ed Parker of Hawaii; many believe it was Parker who, in 1954, initiated the first commercially successful karate school in Provo, Utah. Parker was in the process of obtaining his bachelor's degree in sociology at Brigham Young University.[90] Upon graduation he moved to Pasadena, California, where he opened his *kempo-karate* school in 1956. Here again the semantics of the terms "kempo" and "karate" come into focus. Edward Parker received his *shodan* from the formerly mentioned Mitose graduate, William Chow. Although Parker took additional training in other weaponless arts, he credited his fundamental style of self-defense to Chow. While Parker was called an instructor of karate, he leaned heavily toward the philosophical tradition of James Mitose's *Kosho-ryu kempo.* Thus, if Dr. Mitose's statement and personal conviction is true that *kempo* is intrinsically different from karate, we must conclude that Parker was not a karate instructor in the Okinawan sense; nevertheless his hybrid "karate-kempo-jujutsu" is as effective in combat as any of the purely Okinawan styles being performed today.

Edward Parker's martial art prominence resulted in his being engaged to teach a number of famous people, many of whom were from the film industry such as Elvis Presley, Blake Edwards, Robert Culp, etc. He also appeared in several episodes of the successful television series "I Spy" as one of the "heavies," using his *karate-kempo* to villainous ends. In 1959, the author witnessed a scene being filmed for the movie *Blue Hawaii* with Elvis Presley. Between takes, the rock & roll star was practicing karate stances and *kata* movements with some of the beach boys used for the filming. It was clear he had received some sort of training and the newspapers and local television played this up, claiming he held a *shodan.*

The first "pure" style of karate was introduced to the United States mainland in 1956 by a Japanese national named Tsutomu Ohshima, who opened his school of *Shotokan* karate in Los Angeles.[91] In 1959 Ohshima taught his arts in Brazil and France, finally returning to Japan in 1960. After some time had passed, Ohshima arranged for the well-known Hidetaka Nishiyama to come to California to supervise his *Shotokan* karate school until he could return personally in 1963. After Ohshima returned, Mr. Nishiyama branched off to form his own club. These two men could be called the germinal influence for "pure" karate's great popularity in America today, and combined they head an impressive list of karate experts residing in the United States.

CHAPTER 10

KARATE AND THE LAW

LAW ENFORCEMENT today is saddled with the dilemma of too many guns in the hands of criminals or would-be criminals. America has become a very violent society, and the prognosis for the future does not seem to indicate the coming of a "kinder, gentler America." Crimes involving the use of the martial arts isn't a concern with law enforcement in the 1990s. However, law enforcement must be keenly aware that there are hundreds of thousands of individuals in today's environment that have had some form of martial arts training.

Law Enforcement

At its "grass roots" level, law enforcement by its very nature involves a great deal of physical activity. Much of this activity finds the individual police officer pitted directly against the offender or the suspected offender. Thus, it goes without saying that as a professional group, policemen are more intensely concerned with hand-to-hand combat skills than any other civilian organization. They must, then, devote a serious part of their training to the learning of combat skills that will enable them to handle virtually any violent situation that arises with the greatest dispatch, for self-preservation, for the sake of effective follow-through in situations they feel inclined to move on, and to protect the nearby general public from becoming involved in an uncontrolled melee.

In contemporary law enforcement circles it is felt that a certain portion of the policeman's job is of a public relations nature. Domestic violence is high on the list of criminal activity, which means the policeman on the scene must use nonviolent tactics to defuse potentially dangerous "family" and/or "neighbor" confrontations. That is to say, he is trying to lose the stigma of the heavy-handed, mutton-headed "cop" of yore into the almost genteel diplomatic servant of the people who is capable of preventing crime in as innocuous a manner as possible. This image has been somewhat tarnished by such incidents as the 1991 beating of Rodney King by police officers in Los Angeles County. Despite such lapses of "professionalism," police officers in the United States have reached a higher pinnacle of professional status.

Thus it can be seen that there are many reasons for policemen to improve their weaponless combat skills as well.

Twenty-five years ago, law enforcement agencies were open and willing to allow the taking of photographs of their recruits' unarmed self-defense training sessions. This is not the case today; police practices are now continually under the watchful eye of public interest groups. It might

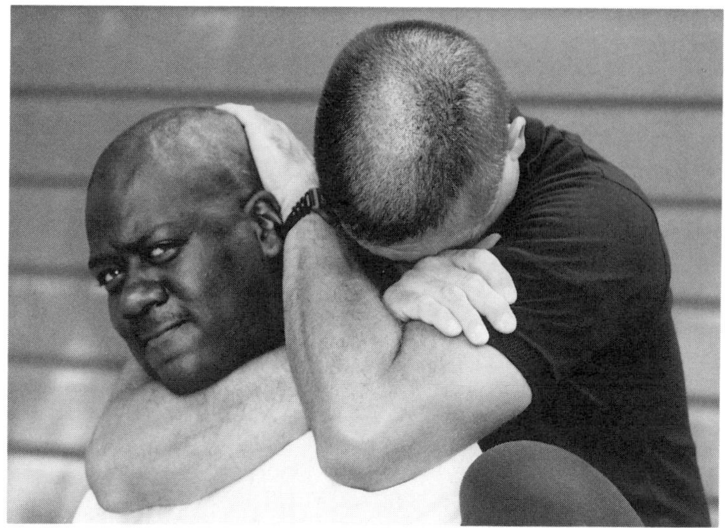

Officer Henry B. Haina, Jr. demonstrates the two-arm carotid restraint on Officer Leon J. Tasor, III. This subjugation hold is in common use by law enforcement agencies worldwide.

be said that after the Rodney King incident, the monitoring of police procedures has become a passion for many.

With the above factors in mind, the author was not surprised when his request to photograph Los Angeles Police Department training sessions was denied. Off the record, a high-ranking officer told the author that such martial arts training sessions are strictly private. This is due in part to litigation concerning the deaths of criminal suspects caused by the use of subjugation holds (i.e., choke holds), take-downs, and other unarmed techniques of restraint. With the police finding themselves under scrutiny more and more, anything that could be interpreted as "police brutality" has become strictly off-limits to anyone outside of the law enforcement community.

Such training could be streamlined considerably if there were a single fighting system that could suffice in all possible emergency situations. Thus far no such system has been found though many have been tried and are being used today. A number of styles have been experimented with and are sometimes adopted in part, but until now have never been seized upon as the "answer" to the need.

Yawara, an ancient Japanese grappling system (see Chap. 6, p. 97), was used experimentally by the Berkeley, California, Police Department under the direction of the late Frank Matsuyama. However, according to a 1966 letter from Berkeley Police Chief A. H. Fording, its usefulness was quite limited for the reasons stated herein:

> This department has not been involved in the teaching of *yawara* for nearly twenty-five years. We were never completely satisfied with it for two basic reasons. First, it was hazardous to our own personnel during the instructional period and we had a number of men seriously injured, some permanently. Second, like so many systems that depend upon leverage, we found that it was hazardous to persons with whom we were dealing. In other words, it was too easy to seriously injure an individual when overcoming some opposition or resistance. At the present time our officers are given a self-defense course that is based primarily upon judo with some modifications as developed by the U.S. military services. It consists primarily of a few simple throws, holds, come-alongs, breaks, and defense against weapons. We have never utilized karate.

Yawara is certainly one of the most exotic of the Asian martial arts to be given a trial in the United States. Such use indicates the extent to which police departments have been going in their search for improved methods.

The "sit-in" tactic used by protesters have brought a new and different task to law enforcement. Officers are now called upon to move bodily great numbers of people who have been specially trained to resist arrest by sitting, squatting, or lying limply in a dead-weighted position. The problem is compounded by onlookers who regularly jump in and try to prevent the police from carting the bodies to police vans. But after learning a few simple ju-jutsu and judo techniques, the police have been able to move these people with a minimum of violence and with much greater alacrity. In its great preoccupation with bodily leverage, judo had been found to be a "gold mine" of seizure methods, take-downs, and "come-along" holds.

Aside from the civil disobedience of the 1960s, the so-called "Bruce Lee Phenomenon" burst on the scene in 1974. His martial arts movies prompted thousands to plunge into training in the various martial arts being taught at that time, namely karate. As the number of students grew, so did the number of schools, clubs, gyms, extension classes, etc. The police were forced to analyze a possible danger to society by semitrained martial artists who could kick, punch, gouge, etc., but who had little of the spiritual training connected with Asian martial arts.

The author was interested in law enforcement's attitude toward karate in the United States so in 1964, he queried twenty-six American cities where karate was practiced in schools or clubs to see if they had formulated a policy concerning the study and application of karate, and also if any of their officers were given special instruction either in karate-associated skills or in defense against an aggressor who is using karate. The results of this questionnaire are incorporated into the chart that follows:

1. Our police department is familiar with karate and its various techniques.

2. The department inspects karate schools in the city for safety measures.
3. Minors are allowed to practice karate without special permission of the police department.
4. There is a regular program where officers learn karate or defense against it.
5. Karate schools teaching the art are licensed by city ordinance.
6. There has been a police officer of this city injured by a suspect using karate.
7. A person using karate in this city would be guilty of attack with a deadly weapon; hence, felonious assault.

Please note that in a number of cities (e.g., Fort Worth, Detroit, Oklahoma City, Jackson, St. Louis, Minneapolis, Denver, Los Angeles, Buffalo, Atlanta, Eugene, Portland, and Honolulu) the reporting agencies initiated special training sessions devoted specifically to handling one's self in situations where the suspect was utilizing karate, or karate-like skills in avoiding arrest. The St. Louis, Missouri, Police Department, in fact, taught *Shorin-ryu* karate to all officer candidates.[1] The Honolulu Police Department, on the other hand, noting the tremendous growth in karate, has offered classes to its officers in defense *against* karate. Police Chief Dan Liu himself is a karate student with Honolulu instructor Edward "Bobby" Lowe.

The State of Hawaii has also pioneered giving karate instruction to the guards in its penal institutions. Ray Belnap, Director of the Hawaii State Correctional System, introduced karate and judo to his guards in the 1960s.[2]

Few cases of assault in which the offender used karate techniques have been noted publicly. However, incidents are known where persons using karate severely injured their nonpracticing opponents, and the details of such incidents were not reported to the investigating authori-

CITY POLICE DEPT.	1	2	3	4	5	6	7
Atlanta, Ga.	✓	×	✓	✓	✓	?	×
Birmingham, Ala.	✓	×	?	×	×	×	✓
Buffalo, N.Y.	✓	×	✓	✓	×	×	*
Chicago, Ill.	✓	×	✓	×	×	×	✓
Denver, Colo.	✓	×	✓	✓	✓	×	*
Des Moines, Iowa	✓	×	?	×	?	×	?
Detroit, Mich.	✓	×	✓	✓	×	×	×
Eugene, Ore.	✓	×	✓	✓	×	×	*
Evanston, Ill.	✓	×	✓	×	×	×	*
Fort Worth, Tex.	✓	×	✓	✓	✓	×	*
Honolulu, Hawaii	✓	×	✓	✓	×	×	×
Indianapolis, Ind.	✓	×	?	×	✓	×	*
Jackson, Miss.	✓	×	?	✓	×	×	✓
Kansas City, Mo.	×	×	✓	×	✓	×	*
Los Angeles, Calif.	✓	×	✓	✓	✓	×	*
Miami, Florida	✓	×	✓	×	✓	×	✓
Minneapolis, Minn.	✓	×	✓	✓	×	**	×
Oklahoma City, Okla.	✓	×	?	✓	✓	×	✓
Philadelphia, Penn.	✓	×	✓	×	✓	×	*
Phoenix, Ariz.	✓	×	✓	×	✓	×	✓
Pittsburgh, Penn.	×	×	?	×	✓	✓	*
Portland, Ore.	✓	×	?	✓	✓	×	*
Raleigh, N.C.	✓	×	×	×	✓	×	✓
Rochester, N Y.	✓	×	✓	×	×	×	✓
St. Louis, Mo.	✓	×	✓	✓	✓	×	✓
Tacoma, Wash.	✓	×	?	×	✓	×	*

✓ Yes
× No
* Depends on circumstances.
** In training.

ties. Also, of the twenty-six cities queried, Pittsburgh had the only police agency that reported an officer injured by a karate-trained suspect. This and other fragmentary reports of karate being used offensively poses the legal question that has been faced by many Asian police agencies: can the martial arts be considered a "weapon" in the sense that their use would constitute an aggravated crime such as felonious assault?

The author found some interesting facts concerning martial arts in the state penal codes of the twenty-one states where questionnaires were sent some thirty years ago. Not one of the states asserted categorically that the use of karate per se in an altercation constituted felonious assault. This contradicts what nine of the cities earlier indicated in answering question number seven.

A possible answer to this inconsistency is that in 1964, when the questionnaires were first directed, karate was relatively new and exotic and law enforcement agencies simply did not have sufficient data concerning it to make bona fide legal judgments. Also, it was law enforcement personnel that answered the 1964 questionnaires and not their prosecutor or district attorney's office.

In the late 1950s and early 1960s, a myth arose concerning karate, namely that a black belt had to register his hands as deadly weapons. This was and still is a myth.

Weapons and the Law

Altough there do not seem to many legal restrictions on the activities of unarmed martial artists, a few states did legislate laws aimed at the use, sale, etc. of certain so-called "karate weapons."

The State of Washington forbids anyone under twenty-one years of age to carry "nun-chu-ka" *(nunchaku)*, throwing stars *(shuriken)*, or any weapon to be used in a martial arts class onto school grounds.

In Michigan, the verdict in a 1976 court case stated that "karate sticks" *(nunchaku)* were not intended as dangerous weapons, and there is no specific limitation of this weapon in the Michigan Penal Code.

Where we see the most precise statutes concerning martial arts weapons is in the state of California. Since 1974, the California Penal Code has prohibited *nunchaku, shuriken,* and "shobi-zue" *(shinobi-zue)* weapons. The Penal Code goes on to define these weapons:

> A 'nunchaku' means an instrument consisting of two or more sticks, clubs, bars, or rods to be used as handles, connected by a rope, cord, wire, or chain, in the design of a weapon used in connection with the practice of a system of self-defense such as karate.
> A 'shuriken' means any instrument, without handles, consisting of a metal plate having three or more radiating points with one or more sharp edges and designed in the shape of a polygon, trefoil, cross, star, diamond, or other geometric shape for use as a weapon for throwing.
> A 'shobi-zue' means a staff, crutch, stick, rod, or pole concealing a knife or blade within it which may be exposed by a flip of the wrist or by a mechanical action.[3]

The law states that "any person in this state who manufactures, . . . imports into the state, keeps for sale, or who gives, lends, or possesses . . . " the above weapons is guilty of a felony, and upon conviction can be imprisoned in a county jail or in state prison for up to one year. There is an exemption for martial arts schools that hold a regulatory or business license.[4]

California goes on to also ban open advertising in magazines, newspapers, etc. the sale of the above weapons that are on the proscribed list of illegal weapons.[5] This is a law that seemingly is not enforced in California. A prime example of this is seen in an ad in the popular magazine *Wushu Kungfu.* There are at least eight hardwood model *nunchaku* for sale, seemingly in defiance of ordinance 12020.5 of the Penal Code. The magazine does run a disclaimer in fine print that says "check Federal, State, and Local Laws. May be illegal in some areas."[6] The sale of *nunchaku* and other weapons is freely advertised in nearly all of the popular martial arts magazines.

Why is this type of advertising legal in California? According to the District Attorney's Office of Los Angeles County, the magazines in question are for national distribution. Because they print a disclaimer that the purchaser must check his or her local ordinances concerning such weapons, they are allowed this type of advertisement.

Despite the fact that hundreds of thousands of individuals have trained in some form of *bu-jutsu* since the late 1950s, martial arts violence has not surfaced in any large degree. Part of this reason can be attributed to the high quality of martial arts training in the United States. Some of the earlier fears of martial artists going "berserk" have been proven to be yet another example of "myths" surrounding karate, kung fu, etc.

The weapon of choice on the street today is a gun, and most likely a semiautomatic weapon capable of tremendous destruction. It has become such a problem in the United States that gun deaths in 1991 in California, New York, Texas, Louisiana, Nevada, Virginia, and the District of Columbia exceeded automobile deaths.[7] With statistics such as these, the legal problems associated with the martial arts have taken a back seat, so to speak, in the arena of law enforcement.

CHAPTER 11

MODERN TRENDS

現代

IN THE FOUR decades of martial arts burgeoning since the 1950s, karate and other Asian martial arts have become household words around the world.

Unfortunately for many in America, interest in karate-like arts is superficial. The difficulty in comprehending the philosophical nuances and meeting the physical challenges of karate are at a price most are not willing to pay. It is not that America lacks spectacular champions and masters, but generally Americans tend to look for the "quick fix" of instant success. If a person pays a *dojo* for karate instruction, he feels that to obtain his money's worth, he must be given timely promotions and eventually the black belt symbolizing mastery of the art—even if it takes no more than one year. As ridiculous as this sounds, it is a theme that has run rampant in many martial arts schools, especially in the 1950s and 1960s. On a more uplifting note, this practice of "degrees for dollars" has become much less prevalent in the 1980s and 1990s. This is because the quality of instruction has greatly improved as many Americans have studied in Asia and Asian instructors have come to the United States with bona fide credentials.

There still are people in Japan, Korea, China, the Philippines, etc. who cling to an almost "medieval" philosophy that total devotion to a skill or art is a necessary experience for developing the "whole man." Certainly, not all Japanese karate enthusiasts are dedicated *budoka* (practitioners of the martial ways). In fact, Japan has her share of dilettantes and quasi-*bu-jutsu* men. There is also a rather pronounced interest in karate by Japan's criminal element—an unfortunate degradation of the art that has largely occurred since the end of World War II—such that karate-trained bodyguards and street toughs are rather common in the Japanese underworld.

Taken overall, however, karate and the other martial arts have had a dynamically positive impact on the culture of Japan. With the numerous martial arts practiced in the schools, universities, and private *dojo,* the fact that violent crime is almost unheard of speaks well for the culture and the influence of the many martial arts masters that have helped frame the nonviolent Japanese lifestyle.

In the 1990s martial arts training, movies, books and magazines, and everything else associated with the Asian fighting arts has become a multibillion dollar industry. Gone, for the most part, are the small *dojo* existing in church basements, YMCAs, and peoples' backyards. Go to a suburban shopping center and one will see the diverse and exotically named schools of karate, tae kwon do, eskrima, etc. Look in the yellow pages of any major city's telephone directory and there is now a separate heading: "Martial Arts."

Another interesting recent development is that many American martial artists are now children. They are taken to the local *dojo* for discipline training and for sport, and they grow up with karate, tae kwon do, etc., in their minds more as a recreational activity than a way of life.

In comparing martial arts development in the United States with that of Japan, the thing that seems not to have accompanied karate, judo, kendo, and aikido on their voyage eastward is the concept of dedication. This has been previously touched on, but little has been said about the effect of Japanese education on martial arts training.

It appears to many educators that the unique quality of Japanese education in general is not gimmickry or methodology, but cultural factors that are ingrained in the Japanese almost from birth. The Japanese family works with the student, shares love with the student, and together they fight trials and tribulations for the student's success. Because of group pressure with other students and teachers, the Japanese student will usually win the "educational battle." Today in America, the student is "on his own" more than ever before. With both parents working just to survive, the American student does not have much parental pressure to succeed in many middle class families, let alone peer pressure to be a top student. This, in part, explains why Asian students, as a whole, do so well academically and in many of their other undertakings. Asian culture puts a premium on education; American culture is more worried about what "goes in the fridge." After thirty years as an educator, the author can vouch for this firsthand. The Japanese educational system instills a stronger will to succeed and enhances their ability to endure the difficulties necessary to achieve their goals.

What does the American look for in martial arts training, if it is not dedicated long-term practice? An advertisement in one of the commonly read men's magazines indicates how some individuals in this country approach the study of karate:

> I'll make you a master of karate. The results of hundreds of years of development in Japan, karate is the secret, Oriental art of deadly self-defense that turns your hands, arms, legs into paralyzing weapons . . . In just two hours after you receive "Super Karate" you will be on your way to being an invincible karate master.[1]

The panacea for the perennial ninety-seven pound weakling of the 1940s was "jiu-jitsu," the first mail-order do-it-yourself bubble. Many currently searching for instant self-confidence look to the martial arts for their salvation, seeing these arts in their brutal aspects, but generally overlooking their philosophical heritage. Granted, we have shown in Chapter 8 that karate's interconnection with the time-honored practices of Buddhism is in most cases superficial. Still, because of the way in which Gichin Funakoshi introduced the art to Japan, there is enough of a philosophical heritage in karate practice to enable one to look upon it as more than an exceptionally effective military skill. Funakoshi was primarily an educator, a former school teacher on Okinawa, who saw karate as the vehicle for educating the whole man—body, mind, and spirit. He was a tireless disciplinarian as well as a master of karate. His emphasis on the moral ethics of karate and his refusal to teach the art to the lay public—he instructed only military personnel and college students—resulted in karate's rather emphatic acceptance into the time-honored family of the Japanese martial arts.[2]

The evolution of karate in Japan has followed two general patterns. Those Okinawan instructors who came first (e.g., Funakoshi, Miyagi, etc.), and taught at a university or college, established the mode for achieving the greatest advancement in the art. The majority of karate students in present-day Japan have emerged from the hallowed institutions of higher learning. These karate practitioners have elevated karate to a plateau rivaling judo, no mean accomplishment when one realizes that judo is commonly thought of by most Japanese (sumo and baseball excepted) and foreigners alike to be Japan's national sport.

The other developmental trend in karate grew from those instructors from Okinawa who did not affiliate themselves with a university. Needing a livelihood, these men opened their karate schools to anyone for the prescribed fee of instruction. The criminal elements using karate today were taught by the instructors who had to admit "all comers" in order to make ends meet financially.

In the 1960s karate first appeared on the American collegiate scene. In September, 1964, the California Institute of Technology in Pasadena, California began regular course instruction in karate. The instructor, Shotokan expert Tsutomu Ohshima, had been teaching karate there in an unofficial capacity since 1958, when he formed what was probably the first college karate club in the United States.

Afer Ohshima's early start, the increase in the number of universities offering some form of the Asian martial arts in the 1990s is astounding. Either in regular PE or through "Extension" classes, judo, t'ai chi ch'uan, tae kwon do, and karate predominate in these areas. An example of this can be found in the Spring 1993 UCLA Extension Catalog showing offerings of Shotokan karate and t'ai chi classes. The screening process for these kinds of classes is such that one can be reasonably sure that he or she won't be ripped off by a charlatan.

In some of the commercial *dojo* the tactics of fly-by-night body building gyms are used to get signatures on contracts that bind the student to a designated number of lessons for exorbitant fees. These schools, run solely for profit, are particularly lax when screening new applicants. On the other hand, there are a few schools that are nonprofit and operate strictly as "clubs." Yet in many instances they too are guilty of teaching karate to undesirables. A sobering aspect of the American karate boom is that there are thousands of potentially dangerous individuals being produced in the United States annually.

As we approach the twenty-first century, the United States has been experiencing a tremendous rise in violent crimes. Guns are the weapon of choice and fortunately one rarely hears of violence committed by martial artists. There have been numerous psychological and sociological studies about violence, but no one can pin down the exact reasons why violence is so endemic in America.

Since the end of World War II, there seems to be lacking a moral code or socially developed norms that allow people to live together peacefully in America. This is not the case in Japan, where criminally perpetrated violent deaths are a fraction of what they are in most of the rest of the world. Social scientists marvel at the Japanese ability to live together in near-perfect harmony despite extremely crowded conditions. Perhaps the positive influence of the many martial arts masters in Japan has in some way contributed to this peacefulness and social order.

Competitive Martial Arts

Martial artists and those interested in Asian fighting arts have contemplated for years how various arts and forms would stand up to each other in real combat. In the 1930s, there were judo versus boxing matches in Hawaii. But to the "purist," contests such as these are a blight on the sacred forms of karate, kung fu, etc. The purist feels that martial arts, especially those associated with Buddhism, must stay free of the contaminating element of actual fighting. They are to be used in self-defense only. The author remembers *kumite* (free sparring) sessions in several karate schools in Honolulu in the 1950s in which contact with your opponent would result in instant disqualification. In practice, hard contact was frowned on, although control of punches and kicks wasn't always carefully observed and sometimes free sparring became full contact. Still, it was felt by the karate "establishment" that one should be able to control blows to a fraction of an inch from an opponent's anatomy, thus allowing referees to score the match.

This changed in the 1970s when tae kwon do instructor Jhoon Rhee introduced padded protective equipment so that semi- or full-contact fighting was possible.[3] For many years now the pads he developed have been used in freestyle semi-contact point fighting tournaments.

In 1979 karate instructor Joko Ninomiya started the Sabaki Challenge, a bare-knuckle tournament in Denver, Colorado.[4] In this event, no hand pads or protective gear other than a mouthpiece and a groin protector are allowed. Rules allow foot sweeps and body punches, but no punches to the head or groin kicks.[5] The popularity of the Sabaki Challenge has grown over the years, with recent attendance figures nearing eight thousand people.

Yoshiji Soeno, founder of the World Karate Association Shidokan, promoted bare-handed fighting tournaments in Japan for over twenty years.[6] In 1991, a Chicago-based Shidokan tournament took place with over two thousand spectators.[7]

Other bare-knuckle tournaments still held in the United States include the New York-based World Open Karate Tournament and the World Kyuk Too Ki full-contact event, which highlights Korean forms.[8] These events have stringent rules for the obvious reason that health and liability are at risk.

In 1993 a further departure on this theme was initiated with the Ultimate Fighting Championship. The brainchild of ju-jutsu instructor Rorion Gracie, it has no point system, no judges, and no draws; victory is obtained when an opponent is knocked out or submits.[9] Various arts (e.g. judo, ju-jutsu, kickboxing, karate, etc.) have been represented in this tournament.

One may argue that "no-holds-barred" fighting proves which are the best forms of combat. Perhaps so, but others argue that this kind of tournament fighting only shows which man or woman is superior at that particular time and place. Either way these are certainly not for the recreational practitioner.

Second- and Third-Generation Schools

The development of Asian martial arts in America has reached the phase where second- and third-generation Western teachers are now opening their own *dojo* and climbing the ranks of their particular arts. The most commonly heard complaint by these American teachers is that skillful as they have become, they rarely get promoted past the fifth degree by their Asian *sensei.* It is also not an uncommon story that some Asian teachers magically gain rank en route to the United States. Some of the earlier Asian martial arts pioneers are shocked at their countrymen's lofty rank when they suddenly appear on the contemporary martial arts scene. This has created confusion and bickering, especially when attempting to form organizations.

Jeff Harris, a second-generation fourth-degree instructor of *hapkido,* owns and operates a school in Pomona,

California. Harris began training in *hapkido* in 1975 with Master Chong Sung Kim, currently a ninth-degree black belt. Master Kim, who arrived in the United States in 1973, is like the legendary Gichin Funakoshi in that he is also a college graduate and demands the highest moral and ethical principles from his graduating black belts. Since 1974, Master Kim has also been teaching at his own school in Alhambra, California.

Ty Aponte, a third-generation fourth-degree instructor of *Shorin-ryu* karate, operates the Defense Arts Center in Upland, California, where several Asian martial arts are taught. Whereas Jeff Harris received his training from Korean Master Kim, Ty Aponte received his black belt from

Ty and Lynn Aponte demonstrate a low posture and side kick from *Shorin-ryu* karate.

another American, Dean Pickard. Pickard received his *shodan* rank from Hawaiian-born Richard Nakano. Nakano in turn studied under Walter Nishioka (see Chap. 9, p. 148), who was also born in Hawaii but had studied *Shorin-ryu* in Japan and Okinawa.[10] So you can see that Pickard *sensei* is even further removed from the "home" of his art than Jeff Harris. This in no way implies that there is something missing or incomplete with those who followed the *Shorin-ryu* way, it only illustrates the depth of karate teaching in America, via Japan and Okinawa.

Spiritualism in Modern Practice

Like the appearance of Zen Buddhism in the 1950s, karate burst on the American scene from the 1960s onward; it hasn't shown any real signs of decline. But in this crescendo, it has all but lost its original identity and has become a "bandwagon" onto which nearly every imaginable Eastern fighting art form has jumped and is clinging precariously. Occasionally, however, a few of the karate-like arts stayed out of the karate camp and succeeded in achieving an identity of their own. One example, t'ai chi ch'uan, an esoteric form of *ch'uan fa*, is being taught in the form of "body awareness" and as a means of reducing stress. This art can be found nationwide and it usually is not combat oriented. One of the earliest pioneers on the United States mainland was Gia-Fu Feng, whose class in the Big Sur area of California worked for nonverbal communication through "meditation in action."[11]

If there was anything in American Asian martial arts practice that approached "cult" status, it was t'ai chi ch'uan in the early 1960s. When karate and *ch'uan fa* slowly surfaced due to films, etc., t'ai chi remained an esoteric and little understood aspect of Chinese martial arts. Part of this was due in no small measure to the "Chinese only" practice previously described. Today, however, this Chinese martial art has made tremendous strides and is practiced by hundreds of thousands of people around the world. To illustrate, in the *Summer 1994 University of California at Riverside Extension Catalog,* there are no less than five different t'ai chi ch'uan classes offered.

Probably ninety percent of t'ai chi practitioners do so for exercise (health reasons); perhaps the other ten percent practicing t'ai chi study its self-defense aspects as part of a generalized kung fu regimen.

Bill Moyers, the noted television journalist, focused several programs on nontraditional health care practices in the 1993 PBS mini-series "Healing and the Mind." Along with Chinese acupuncture and herbal medicine, t'ai chi ch'uan was featured showing its health and fighting aspects. Several remarkable demonstrations of *ch'i* (氣, *ki* in Japanese) were filmed in which a t'ai chi master "moved" numbers of people with this inner power.

If there is anything "mystical" about the Asian martial arts, it is the concept of *ch'i.* It is an energy or force that one utilizes for strength and solidity. This *ki* in Japanese martial arts is seen, or more correctly "heard," in the scream or grunt emitted in kendo, judo, karate, etc. as the practitioner strikes, throws, or punches his opponent. This is the so-called *kiai.* Some call it the "art of the breath."

Bill Moyers seemed amazed and also bemused by the spectacle of a t'ai chi master displaying rigidity and strength in moving five or more people, or in not allowing himself to be moved by a like number of people. A casual observer would find it difficult to ascertain the validity of such demonstrations, and herein lies the confusion many people find in martial arts practice. When does one learn to master this *ch'i* or *ki* power that one hears and reads about? Is there really such a thing as *ch'i* power?

Bill Wallace, one of America's greatest kickboxing champions, does not believe in *ch'i* power. "I don't believe people who claim to use their *ch'i* energy to defeat opponents . . . I haven't found anybody yet who could beat another person by just thinking or talking . . . they can't use *ch'i* to directly attack an opponent."[12]

Until such a time that science can "prove" there is such a thing as *ch'i*, we will have to bide our time and judge this esoteric aspect of Asian martial arts in light of our own experience and philosophy. However, people who initially scoffed at yoga practice and zen meditation found that yogis and zen monks placed under brain-wave (EEG) examinations indeed displayed meditative conditions of calm detachment similar to deep trances. Also, who can forget the horrific scenes of Vietnamese Buddhist monks immolating themselves in political protest over the 1960s reign of South Vietnam's President Ngo Dinh Diem? They sat in the lotus position and burned to death with statuelike demeanor. Be it *ch'i* or Zen, the spiritual and mystical aspects of the martial arts will no doubt continue to be a source of controversy for many years to come.

Yet, karate in America is still by and large identified with brick-breaking and the often brutal fighting competitions that comprise nearly every tournament presented in the United States. The true basis of the art (i.e., *kata*, breathing exercises, and achieving harmony with one's higher nature) are all but forgotten aspects.

In the Movies

With television and motion pictures exploiting the Asian martial arts, it is no small wonder that the public views the karate-like arts as they do. This brings us to the entertainment industry. Hollywood has for better or worse had a great impact on all martial arts in America.

When one speaks or writes about martial arts and movie making, the name of Bruce Lee invariably crops up first and foremost. The author had the good fortune in 1964 to see Bruce Lee in person in Ed Parker's First International Karate Championships at the Long Beach Civic Center. He came on late in the day, demonstrated some kung fu moves and then was motivated by the crowds' appeal to perform with the competition winner, Chuck Norris. There was no official scoring in this demonstration, but the author felt, as did many other witnesses, that Bruce Lee was superior in quickness and technique.

The vehicle that got the American public first interested in Bruce Lee was the 1966 TV series "The Green Hornet." Lee played Kato, the Hornet's valet. With incredible kung fu skill, he punched, kicked, and grunted his way into American homes, and eventually became the byword for the martial arts.

So much has been written about Bruce Lee that it is becoming harder to differentiate fact from fallacy. When someone dies so young (thirty-two), there is natural curiosity. But when a kung fu legend dies mysteriously, everyone speculates. Talk to any martial artist and he will have theories about Lee's death. One theme the author has heard numerous times is that Bruce Lee knew too much, and gave away too much of the Chinese Ancients' secrets and was killed by one of them using a technique of "striking from a distance." This foolish notion has become more widespread now that Brandon Lee, Bruce's actor-son, was killed "accidentally" on the set of his movie *The Crow.* When the father dies at thirty-two and the son at twenty-eight, it is easy to think of curses and omens, and that the family is indeed under a spell.

Bruce Lee made few films, but he started the martial arts movie craze. Investments and returns for these martial arts films runs into the hundreds of millions of dollars. One of today's box office stars is Steven Seagal. This six-foot four-inch tall actor has parlayed his aikido talents into box office gold, albeit through the help of one of his pupils, Michael Ovitz.[13] His first five movies made a total of almost $180 million.[14]

Steven Seagal's background is not easy to trace, though he appears to have trained as a legitimate martial artist. The techniques that he uses are aikido-like in appearance, mixed in with some karate strikes and ju-jutsu joint locks. Seagal's films are very violent and bloody and could possibly become the victim of a growing movement in the US Congress and Hollywood to cut down on violence and mayhem in the entertainment industry.

When it comes to violence on the screen, no one does it better than Chuck Norris. As an Air Force military policeman in Korea, Norris had the opportunity to study *tang soo do,* a type of tae kwon do much indebted to karate. He excelled in this demanding art and achieved his black belt degree in the late 1950s.[15] After Norris was discharged from the Air Force in 1962 he opened his first school in Torrance, California—six more were to follow.[16] When Chuck Norris kept winning tournament after tournament, Hollywood took notice. Also, as a Southern California martial arts instructor, Chuck Norris was able to train some well-known celebrities, which in the long run helped his entry into the action film genre. Norris quit the martial arts gym business in 1975 to concentrate fully on his motion picture career.

David Carradine is a unique case in the martial arts film genre. When the television series "Kung Fu" was in the making in the early 1970s, three actors vied for the role of Kwai Chang Caine: Bruce Lee, William Smith, and

Carradine.[17] Only one of these actors was also a martial artist, the famous Bruce Lee. Lee didn't get the part because he looked "too Chinese;" Smith was rejected because of his fierce countenance; so the door was open for Carradine, who had some background in dance and nothing else akin to martial arts training.

David Carradine grew into his role as the Eurasian Caine, and helped create a very positive image of martial arts that was hitherto absent. "Kung Fu," helped advance the continuing martial arts boom in America.

In the 1990s, Carradine has reprised his role as Caine, though not in the West of the 1850s but in the contemporary world. He has also become more active in martial arts and even helps teach classes in kung fu. It is ironic that Carradine has gone from actor to martial artist, instead of vice versa.

Eclectic Styles

With the variety of martial arts available today, it is not surprising that forms and styles of Asian fighting have merged to form "hybrid" selections. Scan any of the advertisements in the numerous martial arts magazines available today and one will find styles and forms of karate, kung fu, etc. that have been "created" rather recently. Some become popular because martial arts students believe in the efficacy of the form(s); others achieve notoriety because their creator is famous.

Bruce Lee's *Jun Fan* kung fu/*Jeet Kune Do,* which to many is the essence of eclectic fighting forms, is undoubtedly the most widely known of the "newer" martial arts and falls into the latter category. The Republic of China (Taiwan) recognized *Jun Fan* kung fu/*Jeet Kune Do* as an individual art (not a style) on March 27, 1981.[18]

Bruce Lee, movie star and creator of *Jeet Kune Do,* an eclectic martial arts system.

Jeet Kune Do is Bruce Lee's brainchild, born out of his studies of *Wing Chun* kung fu and other arts in Hong Kong. Instead of continuing to teach *Wing Chun* in America, Bruce Lee opted to create his own school of kung fu, that he called "Jun Fan" after his Chinese first name, which means to "return again." Bruce Lee was born in San Francisco and his mother christened him "Jun Fan" in hopes he would return to live in the United States.[19] The name "Bruce" was added later.

Wing Chun/Jun Fan gave Bruce Lee the principles used to create *Jeet Kune Do* in 1967. What he meant by this term (a loose translation means "the way of the intercepting fist") is still argued today by an army of martial artists. In essence, Lee wanted his students to free themselves from the constraints of traditional martial arts; "the ultimate reality," Lee stated, "is the returning to one's primary freedom which is simple, direct, and nonclassical."[20] In other words, do what works for you and don't be tied to rigid traditional forms unless those forms will work best at that particular moment. Bruce Lee's criticism of traditional kung fu did not ingratiate him with the Chinese martial arts community in Hong Kong or the United States. Nonetheless, his concepts paved the way for the many eclectic systems that now abound in the West and allowed martial artists to critically analyze and modernize their arts.

Attempts at Organization

The rather haphazard growth of American karate since 1958 prompted many of its leading figures to attempt formation of a worldwide karate association that would mediate the incessant problems that loomed large on the karate horizon. Many attempts were made and some successes were achieved in the 1960s and 1970s. Much of the problem in organizing such groups was not the lack of zeal or interest by thousands of karateka, but the arguments over "style" that still plague organizational efforts today. With karate's traditional *ryu* coexisting with the eclectic forms created in the 1980s and 1990s, the question of which will be the king of a national karate association continues to this day.

At the end of 1993 an answer loomed on the karate horizon. The World Union of Karate-do Organizations (WUKO), headed by Jacques Delcourt and headquartered in France, and the International Traditional Karate Federation (ITKF), with Los Angeles as its base and the venerable Hidetaka Nishiyama as its chief, have feuded for years over which should lead amateur karate towards the twenty-first century.[21] Both have also aspired for Olympic recognition. This battle between the two groups has hurt karate's chances of Olympic recognition.[22] It appears that WUKO and the ITKF have decided to bury the hatchet to work together.[23] The International Olympic Committee (IOC) has provisionally recognized this merger. Out of this combination of WUKO and the ITKF has emerged the World Karate Federation (WKF), which will consist of two existing disciplines: traditional karate and so-called "general" karate. The ITKF will supervise traditional karate and WUKO, general karate.[24]

The World Tae Kwon Do Federation, on the other hand, has united "most" of the Korean martial artists under its umbrella and has been close to having tae kwon do recognized as an "official" sport in the Olympic competitions (it was a demonstration event previously). *Wushu* kung fu also appears to be heading for Olympic qualification in the year 2000.

As we progress towards the twenty-first century, there are too many millions involved in the Asian martial arts not to have national or worldwide recognition beyond local organizations. Otherwise, the "Balkanization" of karate in the United States and the world will continue to hurt unification efforts and prevent the dream of Olympic karate from being realized.

A Closing Thought

In the final analysis, what have we learned about karate? It is an Asian fighting art, probably of Chinese origin, that reached its zenith in the Ryukyu Islands lying off the coasts of China and Japan. It entered Japan through a marvelous teacher and educator (Gichin Funakoshi) and as they say, the rest is history. The westernization of karate continues to this day, and of all the Asian arts extant today, it is the most widely recognizable.

Karate instructor Tsutomu Ohshima told the author in 1966 that if one hundred karate students in America were "genuine" and honest in their study—in spite of the impostors and charlatans—then karate practice in this country was valid. Today in the 1990s, there are hundreds of thousands of martial artists who train and live the life of the martial artist with varying degrees of dedication. Certainly, America's best are on a par with the best of the rest of the world. America too has matured in many ways, thanks to the martial arts pioneers that brought karate and karate-like arts to these shores.

NOTES

Chapter 1

[1] Pu Chen-chie, *Kuo Chih Chien Luen* (Shanghai, 1936), pp. 12–13.
[2] Gichin Funakoshi, *Karate-jutsu* (Tokyo, 1925), p. 3.
[3] Masatatsu Oyama, *What Is Karate?* (Tokyo, 1958), p. 29.
[4] Hirokata Toyama, *Karate-do* (Tokyo, 1958), p. 23.
[5] *Ibid.*, p. 24.
[6] *Ibid.*
[7] *Ibid.*
[8] *Ibid.*
[9] Hironori Otsuka, *Sekai Dai-Hyakkajiten, VI* (Tokyo, 1955), p. 213.

Chapter 2

[1] The *Lotus Sutra,* author unknown, is called the *Hokke-kyo* in Japanese and *Saddharma Pundarika* in Sanskrit. It is assumed to have been written in Sanskrit somewhere in northern India. The best English translation is William Soothill's *The Lotus of the Wonderful Law.*

[2] William Soothill, *The Lotus of the Wonderful Law* (Oxford, 1930), p. 181.
[3] *Fa Hua San Ch'ing* (Shanghai, 1921), p. 2 of Chapter XIV.
[4] William Soothill, *Dictionary of Chinese Buddhist Terms* (London, 1932). The ideographs 那羅 are read as *nalo* [nah-low] in Mandarin, a transliteration of the Sanskrit *nara.*
[5] *Ibid.*
[6] Yasuhiro Konishi, *Karate Nyumon* (Tokyo, 1958), p. 216. The famous karate master feels that *nara* is a definite link between early Indian fighting and modern karate.
[7] *Hongyo-kyo* is the popular name for the *Busshogyosan* or *Buddha-carita-karya Sutra* in Sanskrit. Its Chinese name is *Pen-hsing Ch'ing* and the original author is unknown, but the work seems to have been written *ca.* 424–453, according to the definitive Japanese Buddhist reference entitled *Bussho Kaisetsu Daijiten.*
[8] Konishi, *Karate Nyumon,* p. 216.
[9] Sir Monier Monier-Williams, *Sanskrit–English Dictionary* (Oxford, 1889), pp. 793–913.
[10] Konishi, *Karate Nyumon,* p. 216.
[11] Louis Frederic, *A Dictionary of the Martial Arts* (Rutland, 1991), p. 93.
[12] Shawn Cephas, "The Root of Warrior Priests in the Martial Arts," *Wushu Kungfu* (Winter, 1994), p. 7.
[13] Frederic, *Dictionary of the Martial Arts,* p. 93.
[14] Cephas, "Warrior Priests," p. 7.
[15] *Ibid.*
[16] *Ibid.*
[17] Chandradhar Sharma, *A Critical Survey of Indian Philosophy* (Delhi, 1964), p. 172.
[18] Cephas, "Warrior Priests," p. 7.
[19] Yasuhiro Konishi, *Yasashii Karate no Narai Kata* (Tokyo, 1957), p. 13.
[20] Konishi, *Karate Nyumon,* p. 216.
[21] Robert Paine and Alexander Soper, *The Art and Architecture of Japan* (Baltimore, 1955), p. 17.

Chapter 3

[1] D. T. Suzuki, *The Essentials of Zen Buddhism* (New York, 1962), p. 106.
[2] Kenneth Ch'en, *Buddhism in China* (Princeton, 1964), p. 351.
[3] Hideo Nakamura, *Sekai Dai-Hyakkajiten, XVIII* (Tokyo, 1955), pp. 487–88.
[4] Chou Hsiang-kuang, *A History of Chinese Buddhism* (Allahabad, India, 1955), p. 91.
[5] Chou Hsiang-kuang, *Dhyana Buddhism, Its History and Teaching* (Allahabad, 1960), p. 20.
[6] E. T. C. Werner, *A Dictionary of Chinese Mythology* (New York, 1961), p. 359.
[7] Chou, *A History of Chinese Buddhism,* p. 91.
[8] Suzuki, *Essentials of Zen Buddhism,* p. 109.
[9] Ch'en, *Buddhism in China,* p. 352.

[10] *Ibid.*
[11] *Ibid.*
[12] *Ibid.*
[13] Chou, *Dhyana Buddhism*, pp. 20–21.
[14] Suzuki, *Essentials of Zen Buddhism*, p. 117.
[15] Ch'en, *Buddhism in China*, p. 352.
[16] *Ibid.*, pp. 483–84.
[17] Pierre Huard and Ming Wong, *La Médecine Chinoise Au Cours Des Siècles* (Paris, 1959), p. 173.
[18] Werner, *Dictionary of Chinese Mythology*, p. 260.
[19] *Ibid.*, p. 268.
[20] *Ibid.*
[21] Huard and Ming, *Médecine Chinoise*; also, Pu Chen-chie, *Kuo Chih*, pp. 12–13; K. Chimin Wong and Wu Lien-teh, *History of Chinese Medicine, Being a Chronicle of Medieval Happenings in China from Ancient Times to the Present Period* (Shanghai, 1936), pp. 72–73.
[22] Konishi, *Yasashii Karate*, p. 13.
[23] Pu, *Kuo Chih*, p. 13.
[24] *Ibid.*
[25] *Ibid.*, p. 13.
[26] *Ibid.*
[27] *Ibid.*
[28] Konishi, *Yasashii Karate*, p. 17.
[29] Pu, *Kuo Chih*, p. 14.
[30] *Ibid.*
[31] *Ibid.*
[32] *Ibid.*
[33] Werner, *Dictionary of Chinese Mythology*, p. 360.
[34] Chou, *Dhyana Buddhism*, p. 23.
[35] Werner, *Dictionary of Chinese Mythology*, p. 360.
[36] Chou, *Dhyana Buddhism*, p. 23.
[37] Werner, *Dictionary of Chinese Mythology*, p. 360.
[38] *Ibid.*
[39] Konishi, *Yasashii Karate*, p. 16.
[40] Carl Glick and Hong Sheng-Hwa, *Swords of Silence: Chinese Secret Societies Past and Present* (New York, 1947), p. 34.
[41] *Ibid.*
[42] Kenneth Scott Latourette, *A Short History of the Far East* (New York, 1959), p. 372.
[43] Li Chien-nung, *Political History of China: 1840–1928* (London, 1956), p. 165.
[44] *Ibid.*
[45] *Ibid.*
[46] " The Boxer Rebellion," *Shanghai Mercury Newspaper*, October, 1900, p. 1.
[47] Li, *Political History*, p. 177.
[48] Frederic, *Dictionary of the Martial Arts*, p. 257.
[49] John Bishop, "Training Behind the Bamboo Curtain," *Secret Fighting Techniques* (January, 1994), p. 14.
[50] Patrick McCarthy, "The Shaolin Temple," *Karate International* (Nov.–Dec., 1993), p. 8.
[51] *Ibid.*, p. 9.
[52] Annbelle A. Udo, "The Birth of WKF," *Wushu Kungfu* magazine (Winter, 1994), pp. 24–25.

Chapter 4

[1] W. Robert Moore, "Angkor, Jewel of the Jungle," *National Geographic Magazine* (April, 1960), pp. 518, 542.

[2] *Ibid.*, p. 524.

[3] *Ibid.*, p. 542.

[4] Letter from W. Robert Moore, Chief Foreign Editorial Staff, *National Geographic Magazine* (November 15, 1965).

[5] *Ibid.*

[6] Moore, "Angkor," p. 524.

[7] *Ibid.*

[8] George M. Kahin (ed.), *Governments and Politics of South-East Asia,* second edition (New York, 1964), p. 597.

[9] *Colliers Encyclopedia, II* (New York, 1961), p. 533.

[10] Kahin, *Governments and Politics,* p. 375.

[11] D.G.E. Hall, *A History of South-East Asia* (London, 1960), p. 170.

[12] *Ibid.*

[13] Frederic, *Dictionary of the Martial Arts,* p. 20.

[14] *Ibid.*

[15] *Ibid.*

[16] *Ibid.*

[17] *Ibid.*

[18] *Ibid.*, p. 253.

[19] After numerous interviews with Vietnamese people in the United States it was clear that the practice of Chinese *ch'uan fa* continued up until several years ago, but it cannot be ascertained how the Communist government is tolerating this.

[20] Peter T. White, "Saigon: Eye of the Storm," *National Geographic Magazine* (June, 1965), p. 870.

[21] Kahin, *Governments and Politics,* p. 375.

[22] Pamphlet from the Muay Thai Academy of America, North Hollywood, California, founded in 1987.

[23] *Ibid.*

[24] interview with Muay Thai Instructor Surapak Jamjuntr, North Hollywood, California, 1994.

[25] Hardy Stockman, *Muay-Thai, The Art of Siamese Unarmed Combat,* unpublished pamphlet, from the Muay-Thai Academy of America, Inc. p. 2.

[26] *Ibid.*

[27] George R. Parulski, et. al., *Karate's Modern Masters* (Chicago, 1985), p. 87.

[28] Frederic, *Dictionary of the Martial Arts,* p. 34.

[29] Kahin, *Governments and Politics,* p. 184.

[30] *Ibid.*

[31] Interview with Rudy Ter Linden and Paul De Thouars, Dutch-Indonesian *pukulan* experts residing in Los Angeles, California, 1966.

[32] *Ibid.*

[33] *Ibid.*

[34] Tape-recorded interview with Abdul Samat, *bersilat* expert, University of Malaya, Kuala Lumpur, Malaysia, 1966.

[35] A.J.G. Papineau, *Kuala Lumpur—Papineau's Guide,* 3rd edition (Singapore, 1964), pp. 54–55.
[36] *Ibid.*
[37] *Ibid.*
[38] *Ibid.*
[39] Letter from Professor Wang Gungwu, Chairman, History Department, University of Malaya, January 28, 1966.
[40] Donn F. Draeger and Robert W. Smith, *Asian Fighting Arts* (Tokyo, 1969), p. 186.
[41] Dan Inosanto, et. al. *The Filipino Martial Arts* (Los Angeles, 1977), p. 10.
[42] John H. Hale, *Age of Exploration* (New York, 1966), p. 97.
[43] Inosanto, *Filipino Martial Arts,* p. 10.
[44] Ciriaco C. Canete and Dionisio A. Canete, *Arnis: Philippine Stick-fighting Art* (Cebu City, 1976), p. 1.
[45] Inosanto, *Filipino Martial Arts,* p. 11.
[46] *Ibid.*
[47] Draeger & Smith, *Asian Fighting Arts,* p. 185.
[48] *Ibid.*
[49] Inosanto, *Filipino Martial Arts,* p. 11.
[50] *Ibid.*
[51] pamphlet by the Ventura Country Eskrima Group & Murrieta Eskrima Academy, *Filipino Martial Arts Seminar: Laban Tulisan System* (Ventura, 1992).
[52] Draeger & Smith, *Asian Fighting Arts,* p. 186.
[53] *Ibid.*, p. 187.
[54] *Ibid.*
[55] Canete & Canete, *Arnis,* p. 2.
[56] Inosanto, *Filipino Martial Arts,* p. 11.
[57] Neofito Santos, *Arnis, The Figure 8 System* (Stockton, 1977), p. 7.
[58] Canete & Canete, *Arnis,* p. 2.
[59] Howard Zinn, *A People's History of the United States* (New York, 1980), p. 306.
[60] *Ibid.*
[61] *Ibid.*, p. 308.
[62] *Ibid.*
[63] Canete & Canete, *Arnis,* p. 2.
[64] Remy Presas, *Modern Arnis, The Filipino Art of Stick Fighting* (Burbank, 1983), p. 2.
[65] Abu Jalmaani and Jun Garcia, *Arnis, Filipino Art of Stick Fighting* (Stockton, 1976), p. 4.
[66] Canete & Canete, *Arnis,* p. 2.

Chapter 5

[1] George H. Kerr, *Okinawa, The History of an Island People* (Tokyo, 1958), p. 22.
[2] *Ibid.*
[3] *Ibid.*
[4] *Ibid.*, p. 29.
[5] *Ibid.*
[6] *Ibid.*, p. 27.
[7] *Ibid.*, p. 40.
[8] *Ibid.*, account following is from this source.
[9] *Ibid.*

[10] Yukitake Yashiro, *Kyoku Ikyohan Karate* (Tokyo, 1958), p. 23.
[11] Reikichi Oya, *Karate No Narai Kata* (Tokyo, 1958), p. 23.
[12] Hironori Otsuka, *Sekai Dai-Hyakkajiten, VI* (Tokyo, 1955), p. 213.
[13] Funakoshi, *Karate-jutsu*, p. 5.
[14] Oya, *Karate No Narai Kata*, p. 8.
[15] Kerr, *Okinawa*, p. 72.
[16] *Ibid.*, p. 66.
[17] *Ibid.*, p. 75.
[18] Oya, *Karate No Narai Kata*, p. 9.
[19] Kerr, *Okinawa*, pp. 83–84.
[20] *Ibid.*, p. 86.
[21] *Ibid.*, pp. 89–90.
[22] *Ibid.*
[23] *Ibid.*, p. 217.
[24] *Ibid.*, pp. 91-92.
[25] Oya, *Karate No Narai Kata*, p. 8.
[26] Kerr, *Okinawa*, pp. 151 ff., 157.
[27] Funakoshi, *Karate-jutsu*, p. 3.
[28] Konishi, *Yasashii Karate*, p. 18.
[29] Yasaburo Shimonaka, *Nippon Dai-Hyakkajiten, V* (Tokyo, 1932), pp. 551–52.
[30] Funakoshi, *Karate-jutsu*, p. 3.
[31] *Ibid.*
[32] *Ibid.*, p. 5.
[33] Oya, *Karate No Narai Kata*, p. 13.
[34] Bruce A. Haines, *Karate and Its Development in Hawaii to 1959* (Honolulu, 1962), p. 62.
[35] Oya, *Karate No Narai Kata*, p. 10.
[36] Funakoshi, *Karate-jutsu*, p. 4.
[37] Shimonaka, *Nippon Dai-Hyakkajiten*, pp. 551–52.
[38] Konishi, *Yasashii Karate*, p. 16.
[39] Oya, *Karate No Narai Kata*, p. 8.
[40] Keishichi Ishiguro, *Karate Hayai Wakari* (Tokyo, 1958), p. 11.
[41] Oya, *Karate No Narai Kata*, p. 10.

Chapter 6

[1] Konishi, *Karate Nyumon*, p. 219.
[2] *Ibid.*
[3] Edwin O. Reischauer, *Japan: Past and Present* (New York, 1946), p. 269.
[4] George Sansom, *A History of Japan to 1334* (Stanford, 1958), p. 423.
[5] Konishi, *Karate Nyumon*, p. 219.
[6] Latourette, *Short History*, p. 199.
[7] Desmond Robbins, "The Throw; The Blow; and The Know," *This Is Japan: 1958* (Tokyo, 1958), pp. 214–17.
[8] Latourette, *Short History*, p. 209.
[9] *Ibid.*, p. 213.
[10] Shunzo Sakamaki, "Ch'en Yuan-pin," *Eminent Chinese of the Ch'ing Period, Vol. I* (Washington, 1943), pp. 106–7.
[11] *Ibid.*
[12] Oyama, *What Is Karate?*, p. 29.
[13] Sakamaki, "Ch'en Yuan-pin," p. 107.
[14] Reverend T. Lindsay and Jigoro Kano, "Jiu Jutsu, the Old Samurai Art of Fighting Without Weapons," *Transactions of the Asiatic Society of Japan, XVI* (Yokohama, 1889), p. 197.
[15] *Ibid.*, p. 193.

[16] *Yoen Jiho Sha* (Okinawan newspaper printed in the Hawaiian Islands), May 1, 1934, p. 3.
[17] *Ibid.*
[18] Yoshimitsu Yamada, *Aikido Complete* (New York, 1969), p. 13.
[19] *Ibid.*, p. 14.

Chapter 7

[1] David Mitchell, *Official WTF Taekwondo* (London, 1986), p. 6.
[2] Draeger & Smith, *Asian Fighting Arts,* p. 71.
[3] Robert Young, "The History and Development of Tae Kyon," *Journal of Asian Martial Arts,* Volume 2 Number 2, 1993, p. 46.
[4] Richard Chun, *Tae Kwon Do, Korean Art of Self-Defense* (New York, 1969), p. 10.
[5] Norman Kotker (ed.), *The Horizon History of China* (New York, 1969), p. 140.
[6] Richard Chun, *Tae Kwon Do,* p. 11.
[7] Draeger & Smith, *Asian Fighting Arts,* p. 70.
[8] *Ibid.*
[9] Hee Il Cho, *The Complete Tae Kwon Do Hyung* (Los Angeles, 1984), p. 15.
[10] Draeger & Smith, *Asian Fighting Arts,* p. 70.
[11] Hee, *Complete Tae Kwon Do,* p. 15.
[12] Draeger & Smith, *Asian Fighting Arts,* p. 70.
[13] *Ibid.*, p. 71.
[14] *Ibid.*
[15] Cho, *Complete Tae Kwon Do,* p. 15.
[16] *Ibid.*
[17] Woo-Keun Han, *The History of Korea* (Seoul, 1970), p. 60.
[18] *Ibid.*
[19] *Ibid.*
[20] Mitchell, *Official WTF Taekwondo,* p. 7.
[21] Bong-Youn Choy, *Korea: A History* (Tokyo, 1971), p. 29.
[22] *Ibid.*
[23] Draeger & Smith, *Asian Fighting Arts,* p. 72.
[24] Chun, *Tae Kwon Do,* p. 11.
[25] Mitchell, *Official WTF Taekwondo,* p. 7.
[26] Mitchell, *Ibid.*, p. 8.
[27] Chun, *Tae Kwon Do,* p. 10.
[28] *Ibid.*
[29] Mitchell, *Official WTF Taekwondo,* p. 8.
[30] Young, "History and Development," p. 51.
[31] Robert K. Spear, *Hapkido, the Integrated Fighting Art* (Burbank, 1988), p. 3.
[32] *Ibid.*
[33] *Ibid.*, p. 4.
[34] *Ibid.*, p. 5.
[35] Mitchell, *Official WTF Taekwondo,* p. 8.
[36] named so for the T'ang dynasty in China (618–907)
[37] Chun, *Tae Kwon Do,* p. 11.
[38] Cho, *Complete Tae Kwon Do,* pp. 16–17.

[39] *Ibid.*
[40] Robert W. Young, "History and Development" and Willy Pieter, "Korean Martial Arts," *Journal of Asian Martial Arts,* Vol. 3, No. 1. p. 83 ff., 1994.
[41] *Ibid.*

Chapter 8

[1] Yashiro, *Kyoiku Ikyohan Karate,* p. 25.
[2] Alan Watts, *The Way of Zen* (New York, 1957), p. 70.
[3] D.T. Suzuki, *Zen Buddhism* (New York, 1956), p. 290.
[4] *Ibid.,* p. 289.
[5] *Ibid.,* p. 53.
[6] Watts, *Way of Zen,* p. 86.
[7] *Ibid.,* p. 87.
[8] Konishi, *Yasashii Karate,* p. 16.
[9] *Ibid.*
[10] Wolfram Eberhard, *History of China* (Berkeley, 1956), p. 142.
[11] *Ibid.,* p. 111.
[12] Pu, *Kuo Chih,* p. 13.
[13] Li, *Political History,* p. 166.
[14] Suzuki, *Zen Buddhism,* p. 288.

Chapter 9

[1] *Colliers Encyclopedia, XIX* (New York, 1961), pp. 10–11.
[2] Latourette, *Short History,* p. 386.
[3] Gunther Barth, *Bitter Strength, A History of the Chinese in the United States, 1850–1870* (Cambridge, Massachusetts, 1964), p. 110.
[4] *Ibid.,* p. 78.
[5] *Ibid.,* p. 80.
[6] *Ibid.,* pp. 94–95.
[7] *Ibid.*
[8] *Ibid.,* p. 102.
[9] *Ibid.*
[10] Calvin Lee, *Chinatown,* U.S.A., (New York, 1965), p. 36.
[11] Barth, *Bitter Strength,* p. 103.
[12] *Ibid.*
[13] *Ibid.*
[14] *Ibid.,* p. 106
[15] Lee, *Chinatown,* p. 35.
[16] Tan Lo, "Ket On Association," *Pan Pacific Magazine* (October–December 1937), p. 49.
[17] Interview with Hin Sum Young, executive secretary of United Chinese Society, Honolulu, May 1962.
[18] Chung Wo Au, "See Yap Benevolent Society," *Pan Pacific Magazine* (October–December 1937), p. 49.
[19] Young interview.
[20] *Ibid.*
[21] Lee, *Chinatown,* p. 61.
[22] Young interview.
[23] Interview with Tinn Chan Lee, May 1962.
[24] *Ibid.*
[25] *Ibid.*
[26] *Ibid.*
[27] Kiyoshi Ikeda, *A Comparative Study of Mental Illness Differences Among Okinawan and Naichi Japanese in Hawaii* (Honolulu, 1955), p. 25.
[28] *Ibid.,* p. 24.
[29] *Ibid.*
[30] Latourette, *Short History,* p. 530.

[31] Earnest K. Wakukawa, *A History of the Japanese People in Hawaii* (Honolulu, 1938), p. 28.
[32] Latourette, *Short History,* p. 530.
[33] *Ibid.*
[34] *Ibid.*
[35] *Ibid.*
[36] Wakukawa, *History of the Japanese People,* p. 143.
[37] *Ibid.*
[38] Claude A. Buss, *The Far East* (New York, 1960), p. 371 ff.
[39] Haines, *Karate and Its Development,* p. 62.
[40] *Ibid.*, p. 63.
[41] *Ibid.*
[42] *Jitsugyo no Hawai* (May 1927), p. 50.
[43] Haines, *Karate and Its Development,* p. 65.
[44] *Ibid.*
[45] *Ibid.*
[46] *Ibid.*, p. 66.
[47] *Ibid.*
[48] *Ibid.*
[49] *Ibid.*
[50] *Ibid.*
[51] *Ibid.*, p. 67.
[52] *Ibid.*
[53] *Ibid.*
[54] Interview with Chinei Kinjo, editor of *Yoen Jiho Sha,* April 1959, May 1962.
[55] *Ibid.*
[56] *Yoen Jiho Sha,* May 1, 1934, p. 3.
[57] *Ibid.*
[58] *Yoen Jiho Sha,* May 29, 1934, p. 3.
[59] Haines, *Karate and Its Development,* p. 71.
[60] *Ibid.*
[61] Interviews with Dr. James M. Mitose, Los Angeles, California, 1958–60, 1966.
[62] *Ibid.*
[63] *Ibid.*
[64] *Ibid.*
[65] *Ibid.*
[66] James M. Mitose, *What Is Self-Defense?* (Honolulu, 1953), p. 6.
[67] Mitose interviews.
[68] Mitose, *What Is Self-Defense?,* p. 4.
[69] Mitose interviews.
[70] Haines, *Karate and Its Development,* p. 75.
[71] *Ibid.*, p. 77.
[72] *Ibid.*, p. 76.
[73] *Ibid.*, pp. 78–79.
[74] *Ibid.*, p. 81.
[75] *Ibid.*
[76] *Ibid.*, p. 82.
[77] *Ibid.*, p. 83.
[78] *Ibid.*
[79] *Ibid.*, p. 89.
[80] *Ibid.*, p. 90.
[81] Linda Lee and Tom Bleecker, *The Bruce Lee Story,* (Burbank, 1989), p. 49.
[82] Interviews with Wong Ark Yuey, 1965–66
[83] Lee, *The Bruce Lee Story,* p. 62
[84] *Ibid.*
[85] *Ibid.*
[86] *Ibid.*, p. 53
[87] Interview with Tsutomu Ohshi-

ma, *Shotokan* karate expert, Los Angeles, California, June 1966.
[88] *Ibid.*
[89] George R. Parulski, et al., *Karate's Modern Masters,* (Chicago, 1985), p. 8.
[90] Interview with Edward Parker, Pasadena, California, 1958, 1966.
[91] Ohshima interview.

Chapter 10

[1] Questionnaire received from Robert L. Berton, director of Public Relations, City of St. Louis Police Department, April 1966.
[2] Alf Pratte, "Prison Guards Get New Weapons: Karate and Judo," *Black Belt* magazine (August 1966), p. 15.
[3] *Deering's Penal Code* (San Francisco, 1992), pp. 1061–1062.
[4] *Ibid.*, p. 1059.
[5] *Ibid.*, p. 1063.
[6] *Wushu Kungfu,* (Winter, 1994), Inside Front Cover.
[7] *Inland Valley Daily Bulletin* (January 28, 1994), p. 1A.

Chapter 11

[1] Cited in *Sir* magazine (February, 1964), p. 63.
[2] Interview with Ohshima, July 1966.
[3] Robert W. Young, "Bare Knuckle Bouts," *Black Belt* magazine (February, 1994), p. 51.
[4] *Ibid.*
[5] *Ibid.*
[6] *Ibid.*
[7] *Ibid.*
[8] *Ibid.*
[9] *Ibid.*
[10] Telephone interview with Dean Pickard, August 10, 1993.
[11] *Los Angeles Times,* April 24, 1966, p. 1 Section C.
[12] *Black Belt* magazine (February, 1994), p. 10
[13] *Los Angeles Times,* October 20, 1992, p. 1 Section F.
[14] *Ibid.*
[15] Chuck Norris & Joe Hyams, *The Secret of Inner Strength—My Story* (Boston, 1988), p. 37.
[16] George R. Parulski, et al., *Karate's Modern Masters,* p. 14.
[17] David Carradine, *Spirit of Shaolin* (Boston, 1991), p. 18.
[18] Chris Kent and Tim Tackett, *Jun Fan/Jeet Kune Do: The Textbook* (Los Angeles, 1988), p. 8.
[19] Linda Lee and Tom Bleecker, *The Bruce Lee Story* (Burbank, 1989), p. 20.
[20] *Ibid.*, p. 9.
[21] Jim Coleman, "Questions and Answers With WUKO's Head Man," *Black Belt* magazine (September, 1993), pp. 30–31.
[22] Interview with Ty Aponte, August 9, 1993.
[23] *Black Belt* magazine, (February, 1994), p. 13.
[24] *Ibid.*

BIBLIOGRAPHY

The bibliography is divided into the following categories: Primary Written Sources, General Written Works, Newspapers, Magazines, Interviews, Letters, Questionnaires, Theses, and Special Sources.

Primary Written Sources

Canete, Cirriaco E. and Dionisio A. Canete: *Arnis: Philippine Stickfighting Art,* Cebu City , 1976

Carradine, David: *Spirit of Shaolin,* Boston, 1991

Cho, Hee Il: *The Complete Tae Kwon Do Hyung,* Los Angeles, 1984

Chun, Richard: *Tae Kwon Do, Korean Art of Self-Defense,* Santa Clarita, 1975

Draeger, Donn F. and Robert W. Smith: *Asian Fighting Arts,* Tokyo, 1969

Frederic, Louis: *A Dictionary of the Martial Arts,* Rutland, 1991

Funakoshi, Gichin: *Karate-jutsu,* Tokyo, 1925

Harrison, Ernest J.: *Manual of Karate,* London, 1959

Inosanto, Dan, et. al.: *The Filipino Martial Arts,* Los Angeles, 1977
Jalmaani, Abu and Jun Garcia: *Arnis, Filipino Art of Stick Fighting,* Stockton, 1976
Kent, Chris and Tim Tackett: *Jun Fan/Jeet Kune Do: The Textbook,* Los Angeles, 1988
Konishi, Yasuhiro: *Karate-do Nyumon,* Tokyo, 1958
———: *Karate Nyumon,* Tokyo, 1958
———: *Yasashii Karate no Narai Kata,* Tokyo, 1957
Lee, Linda and Tom Bleecker: *The Bruce Lee Story,* Burbank, 1989
Mitchell, David: *Official WTF Taekwondo,* London, 1986
Mitose, James M.: *What Is Self-Defense?,* Honolulu, 1953
Nishiyama, Hidetaka and Richard Brown: *Karate, the Art of Empty Hand Fighting,* Tokyo, 1960
Norris, Chuck & Joe Hyams: *The Secret of Inner Strength—My Story,* Boston, 1988
Oya, Reikichi: *Karate no Narai Kata,* Tokyo, 1958
Oyama, Masatatsu: *What Is Karate?,* Tokyo, 1958
———: *What Is Karate?* (revised edition), Tokyo, 1959
Parulski, George R., et. al.: *Karate's Modern Masters,* Chicago, 1985
Presas, Remy: *Modern Arnis, The Filipino Art of Stick Fighting,* Burbank, 1983
Pu Chen-chie: *Kuo Chih Jien Luen,* Shanghai, 1936
Santos, Neofito: *Arnis, the Figure 8 System,* Stockton, 1977
Spear, Robert K.: *Hapkido, the Integrated Fighting Art,* Burbank, 1988
Toyama, Hirokata: *Karate-do,* Tokyo, 1958
Yamada, Yoshimitsu: *Aikido Complete,* New York, 1969
Yashiro, Yukitake: *Kyoku Ikyohan Karate,* Tokyo, 1958

General Written Works

Barth, Gunther: *Bitter Strength, A History of the Chinese in the United States, 1850–1870,* Cambridge, Massachusetts, 1964
Blakney, R. B.: *Tao Te Ching* (translation from the Chinese), New York, 1955
Bong-Youn Choy: *Korea: A History,* Tokyo, 1971
Borton, Hugh: *Japan,* New York, 1950
Burney, David, et. al.: *America, A Portrait in History,* Englewood Cliffs, 1974
Buss, Claude A.: *The Far East,* New York, 1960

Ch'en, Kenneth: *Buddhism in China,* Princeton, 1964
Chou Hsiang-kuang: *A History of Chinese Buddhism,* Allahabad, India, 1955
———: *Dhyana Buddhism, Its History & Teaching,* Allahabad, 1960
Conze, Edward: *Buddhism,* Oxford, 1957
Creel, H. G.: *Chinese Thought, from Confucius to Mao Tse-tung,* New York, 1953
Deering's Penal Code, San Francisco, 1992
Dumoulin, Heinrich: *A History of Zen Buddhism,* New York, 1963
———: *The Development of Zen After the Sixth Patriarch in the Light of Mumonkan,* New York, 1953
Eberhard, Wolfram: *History of China,* Berkeley, 1956
Fa Hua San Ch'ing, Shanghai, 1936
Fang, Chao-ying (ed.): *Eminent Chinese of the Ch'ing Period* (3 vols.), Washington, D.C., 1943
Fitzgerald, C. P.: *China, A Short Cultural History* (third edition), New York, 1965
Glick, Carl and Hong Sheng-Hwa: *Swords of Silence: Chinese Secret Societies Past and Present,* New York, 1947
Goodrich, L. Carrington: *A Short History of the Chinese People* (third edition), New York, 1959
Goshal, Kumar: *People of India,* New York, 1944
Hall, D. G. E.: A *History of South-East Asia,* London, 1960
Harrison, Ernest J.: *The Fighting Spirit of Japan,* London, 1913
Heibonsha: *Daijiten* (26 vols.), Tokyo, 1932
Huard, Pierre and Ming Wong: *La Médecine Chinoise Au Cours Des Siècles,* Paris, 1959
Inouye, Kenkai: *Hokkekyo Kowa,* Tokyo, 1939
Ishiguro, Keishichi: *Karate Hayai Wakari,* Tokyo, 1958
Kahin, George M. (ed.): *Governments and Politics of South-East Asia* (second edition), New York, 1964
Kerr, George H.: *Okinawa: A History of an Island People,* Tokyo, 1958
Kotker, Norman (ed.): *The Horizon History of China,* New York, 1969
Kuno, Takeshi: *Album of Japanese Prints: Kamakura Period,* Tokyo, 1932
Latourette, Kenneth S.: *A Short History of the Far East,* New York, 1959
Lee, Calvin: *Chinatown, U.S.A.,* New York, 1965
Li Chien-nung: *Political History of China: 1840–1928,* London, 1956
Lind, Andrew: *An Island Community,* Chicago, 1938

———: *Hawaii's Japanese,* New Jersey, 1946
Makiyama, Thomas H.: *The Techniques of Aikido,* Honolulu, 1960
Mochizuki, Shinkyo: (ed.) *Bukkyo Daijiten,* Tokyo, 1935
Monier-Williams, Sir Monier: *Sanskrit-English Dictionary,* London, 1898
Monumenta Nipponica (20 vols.), Tokyo, 1965
Natori, Yonosuke: *Mai-Chi-Shan Caves,* Tokyo, 1957
Ono, Genmyo: (ed.) *Bussho Kaisetsu Daijiten,* Tokyo, 1935
Pan Ku: *History of the Former Han Dynasty* (2 vols.), translation from the Chinese by Homer H. Dubbs, Baltimore, 1938
Papineau, A.J.G.: *Kuala Lumpur—Papineau's Guide,* Singapore, 1964
Reischauer, Edwin O.: *Japan, Past and Present,* New York, 1946
Robbins, Desmond: "The Throw; The Blow; and The Know," *This Is Japan: 1958,* Tokyo, 1958
Sansom, George: *A History of Japan to 1334,* Stanford, 1958
Sargeant, J. A.: *Sumo: The Sport and the Tradition,* Tokyo, 1959
SCAP: *Political Reorientation of Japan,* Washington, D. C., 1943
Sekai Dai-Hyakkajiten (31 vols.), Tokyo, 1955
Sen, Gertrude: *Pageant of India's History,* New York, 1948
Shimmura, Izuru (ed.): *Kaihyo Sosho* (6 vols.), Tokyo, 1928
Shimonaka, Yasaburo (ed.): *Dai Hyakkajiten* (27 vols.), Tokyo, 1932
———: *Shiseki Kaidai,* Tokyo, 1936
———: *Kokushi Jiten* (4 vols.), Tokyo, 1932
Soothill, William: *Dictionary of Chinese Buddhist Terms,* London, 1932
———: *The Lotus of the Wonderful Law,* Oxford, 1930
Soper, Alexander and Robert Paine: *Art and Architecture of Japan,* Baltimore, 1955
Suzuki, D. T.: *Essays in Zen Buddhism,* New York, 1956
———: *The Essentials of Zen Buddhism,* New York, 1962
———: *The Lankavatara Sutra,* London, 1932
Transactions of the Asiatic Society of Japan (first series, 50 vols.)
Wakukawa, Ernest K.: *A History of the Japanese People in Hawaii,* Honolulu, 1938
Watts, Alan W.: *The Way of Zen,* New York, 1957
Werner, E. T. C.: *A Dictionary of Chinese Mythology,* New York, 1961
Wong, K. Chimin and Wu Lien-teh: *History of Chinese Medicine, Being a Chronicle of Medieval Happenings in China from Ancient Times to the Present Period,* Shanghai, 1936
Woo-Keun Han: *The History of Korea,* Seoul, 1970

Zinn, Howard: *A People's History of the United States,* New York, 1980
Zurcher, Erik: *Buddhism,* New York, 1962
———: *The Buddhist Conquest of China: The Spread and Adaptation of Buddhism in Early Medieval China,* Leiden, 1959

Newspapers

Shanghai Mercury News: Shanghai, 1900
Honolulu Advertiser: Honolulu, 1933, 1934, 1959–1962
Honolulu Star Bulletin: Honolulu, 1959–1962
Inland Valley Daily Bulletin: Los Angeles, 1994
Los Angeles Times: Los Angeles, 1966–94
Nippu Jiji: Honolulu, 1933–1935
Yoen Jiho Sha: Koloa, Kauai (Hawaii), 1933–1935

Magazines

Asia Scene: 1959
Black Belt magazine: 1962–66, 1993, 1994
Jitsugyo no Hawai: May 1927, 1933
Journal of Asian Martial Arts: 1993, 1994
Karate International magazine: 1993
Life magazine: 1947, 1966
Look magazine: 1961
National Geographic Magazine: 1960, 1964, 1965
Pan Pacific magazine: 1937
Physical Education Research Quarterly: 1963
Secret Fighting Techniques: 1994
Sir magazine: 1964
Wushu Kungfu magazine: 1994

Interviews

Aponte, Ty: Karate instructor, 1993, 1994
Bingo, Thomas: Karate instructor, 1959
Chow, William: *Kempo-karate* instructor, 1955, 1959
De Thouars, Paul: Indonesian martial arts expert, 1965, 1966
Gill, Lorin: Program director, Palama Settlement, 1959
Harris, Jeff: *Hapkido* Instructor, 1993
Hasegawa, Yoshio: Assistant Chief of Police, Honolulu, 1959
Higa Watoku: Okinawan immigrant and karate practitioner, 1959

Hu, William: *Ch'uan fa* instructor, 1959
Jamjuntr, Surapak: *Muay Thai* instructor
Kanashiro, Dr. James Z.: Okinawan-American citizen, 1962
Kerr, George: Authority on Okinawa and author, 1958
Kim, Richard: Karate instructor, 1959
Kinjo, Chinei: Editor of Okinawan-American newspaper, 1959, 1962
Kobayashi, Mitsugi: Karate instructor, 1959
Kubo, Earl: Honolulu Police Department, 1962
Lee, Tinn Chan: *Ch'uan fa* instructor, 1962
Lowe, Edward: Karate instructor, 1959
Matsumoto, James: Karate student, 1959
Meyer, Robert: Physical director, Nuuanu YMCA, 1962
Mitose, Dr. James M.: *Kempo* instructor and author, 1958–1960, 1966
Miyasaki, George: Karate instructor, 1959, 1961
Miyashiro, Thomas: Karate instructor, 1962
Murakami, Kenneth: Karate instructor, 1959, 1961
Murasaki, Yoshio: Karate instructor, 1962
Niiya, Brian: staff member, Japanese-American Museum, 1994
Ohshima, Tsutomu: Karate instructor, 1966
Okubo, Shungo: Executive secretary, Moiliili Community Association, 1962
Oshiro, Masaichi: Karate instructor, 1955, 1959
Parker, Edward: *Kempo-karate* instructor, 1958, 1966
Pickard, Dean: Karate instructor, 1993
Shimomi, Carlton: Karate instructor, 1959
Tackett, Tim: *Eskrima* and *Jeet Kune Do* instructor, 1993
Ter Linden, Rudy: Indonesian martial arts expert, 1965, 1966
Teruya, Kiso: Okinawan-American resident of Hawaii, 1962
Wong Ark Yuey: *Ch'uan fa* instructor, 1965
Yamaguchi, Paul: Karate instructor, 1959
Young, Hin Sum: Executive secretary, United Chinese Society, 1962
Young, Thomas: *Kempo* instructor, 1959, 1962

Letters

Arika, Hitoshi: Doshisha University Karate Club, 1966
Fukuda, Tokushi: President, Kagoshima University, 1966
Fujimura, Toru: Head, Student Affairs, Ibaraki University, 1966

Furukawa, Noboru: Office of Student Personnel, Rikkyo University, 1966
Hasegawa, Shuji: Office of the President, Gumma University, 1966
Inoue, Akio: Overseas Missions Department, Tenri University, 1965
Moore, W. Robert: Chief, Foreign Editorial Staff, *National Geographic Magazine,* 1965
Karate Dobu: Nihon University, 1966
Karate Dobu: Tohoku University, 1966
Wang Gungwu: Head, Department of History, University of Malaya, 1966

Questionnaires
(Police Departments)
Atlanta (Georgia): Lt. R. M. Lane, Training Division
Birmingham (Alabama): Capt. Jack A. Warren, Personnel and Training
Buffalo (New York): Sgt. James H. Goss, Assistant Police Instructor
Chicago (Illinois): Robert E. McCann, Director of Training
Denver (Colorado): Lt. A. Dill, Director of Training
Des Moines (Iowa): Lt. B. B. Wallace
Detroit (Michigan): Lt. Bernard Winckoski
Eugene (Oregon): Lt. William W. Smith
Evanston (Illinois): Lt. Robert Witt, Planning and Research
Fort Worth (Texas): J. P. Moore, Planning Officer
Honolulu (Hawaii): Lt. G. Caringer, Planning and Training Division
Indianapolis (Indiana): Deputy Chief of Police, O. K. Gleich
Jackson (Mississippi): Chief of Police, W. D. Rayfield
Kansas City (Missouri): Lt. Marion L. Cooley, Planning and Research
Los Angeles (California): Lt. Ted Morton
Miami (Florida): Lt. Kenneth E. Fox
Minneapolis (Minnesota): Superintendent of Police Calvin F. Hawkinson
Oklahoma City (Oklahoma): Sgt. Lon L. Heggy, Planning and Research
Philadelphia (Pennsylvania): Capt. Michael Roxinon
Phoenix (Arizona): Sgt. B. Thompson, Public Information
Pittsburgh (Pennsylvania): Sgt. E. A. Patterson, Personnel Division
Portland (Oregon): Lt. J. E. Harvey, Training Division
Raleigh (North Carolina): Lt. C. H. Haswell, Director of Personnel
Rochester (New York): Deputy Chief of Police Harry E. Griswald
St. Louis (Missouri): Robert L. Berton, Director of Public Relations

Tacoma (Washington): Police Department

Theses

Haines, Bruce A.: *Karate and Its Development in Hawaii to 1959,* University of Hawaii, 1962

Ikeda, Kiyoshi: *A Comparative Study of Mental Illness Differences Among Okinawan and Naichi Japanese in Hawaii,* University of Hawaii, 1955

Lin, Ronald: *Sunyata: Part II,* Ryukoku University (Kyoto, Japan), 1955

Special Sources

Film: *Beyond the Great Wall*

Film: *Paths of Nirvana*

Letter: Masatatsu Oyama to Edward Lowe, 1958

Pamphlet: Muay Thai Academy of America, Inc.

Pamphlet: Hardy Stockman, *Muay-Thai, The Art of Siamese Unarmed Combat*

Pamphlet: *Filipino Martial Arts Seminar: Laban Tulisan System,* printed by the Ventura Country Eskrima Group and Murrieta Eskrima Academy, Ventura, 1992

Tape Recorded Interview: *Bersilat* expert Abdul Samat, from Dr. B. C. Stone, University of Malaya, 1966

TV Mini-series: "Healing and the Mind," 1993

GLOSSARY-INDEX

Other Titles in the Tuttle Library of Martial Arts

BEGINNING T'AI CHI *by Tri Thong Dang*

T'ai Chi is a holistic method of self-healing, moving meditation, and a philosophical way of life. This handy guide introduces the "Simplified T'ai Chi" form, which was specifically designed for beginners by China's Ministry of Physical Culture and Sports.

THE ESSENCE OF OKINAWAN KARATE-DO *by Shoshin Nagamine*

A rich source on the technique and philosophy of pure Okinawan karate. The only book in English with photographs of one of the legendary prewar masters demonstrating the correct way to do Okinawan karate, *The Essence of Okinawan Karate-do* is the bridge between karate's legendary past and the practitioners of today.

ESSENTIAL SHORINJIRYU KARATEDO *by Masayuki Kukan Hisataka*

A well-rounded guide to this highly innovative and effective martial art. Describing preset forms, fighting combinations, and weapons, it is an excellent introduction to this comprehensive fighting system.

FILIPINO MARTIAL ARTS: CABALES SERRADA ESCRIMA *by Mark V. Wiley*

An excellent introduction to this deadly but graceful Filipino art of armed and unarmed combat. Packed full of information on the techniques, tactics, philosophy, spirituality, and history of the Filipino martial arts, this book is a vital addition to any martial arts library.

THE HAND IS MY SWORD: A KARATE HANDBOOK *by Robert A. Trias*

The history, the fundamentals, and the basic techniques and katas are brought to life by over 600 illustrations in this book, which teaches that to master others one must first master oneself.

KARATE: THE ART OF "EMPTY-HAND" FIGHTING
by Hidetaka Nishiyama and Richard C. Brown

A highly acclaimed, unexcelled treatment of the techniques and principles of karate. Includes over 1,000 easy-to-follow illustrations and a thorough review of the history and organization of the art.

SECRETS OF THE SAMURAI *by Oscar Ratti and Adele Westbrook*

"Ratti and Westbrook have captured the breadth and depth of feudal Japanese *bujutsu* and its modern progeny. Anyone with a genuine interest in the roots of Japanese military tradition and martial arts should have this book." —*The Journal of Asian Martial Arts*

SHAOLIN: LOHAN KUNG FU
by P'ng Chye Khim and Donn F. Draeger

A clearly written manual giving detailed explanations of the special elements of South China's Lohan style of Shaolin, including the Lohan pattern in both solo and partner forms.

TAE KWON DO: SECRETS OF KOREAN KARATE
by Sihak Henry Cho

This book teaches Tae Kwon Do, probably the strongest form of self-defense known. This Korean form of karate is highly competitive, and its practice is one of the best ways to achieve mental and physical fitness.

THE WEAPONS AND FIGHTING ARTS OF INDONESIA
by Donn F. Draeger

Discover the ancient and modern combative forms of the Indonesian archipelago. As varied as the islands themselves, the styles described in this classic work include mysterious and deadly unarmed and weapons arts.

ZEN SHAOLIN KARATE: THE COMPLETE PRACTICE, PHILOSOPHY & HISTORY *by Nathan Johnson*

The ultimate interpretation of karate forms. A book that breaks the barriers separating karate, kung fu, and aikido, it revolutionizes the way preset forms are applied in all karate styles.